COMMUNICATING WITH DATABASES IN NATURAL LANGUAGE

M. WALLACE, BA, MA, MSc, PhD
Software Designer/Implementor
International Computers Limited
Reading, Berkshire, England

ELLIS HORWOOD LIMITED
Publishers · Chichester

Halsted Press: a division of
JOHN WILEY & SONS
New York · Chichester · Brisbane · Toronto

First published in 1984
Reprinted in 1985 by
ELLIS HORWOOD LIMITED
Market Cross House, Cooper Street, Chichester, West Sussex, PO19 1EB, England

The publisher's colophon is reproduced from James Gillison's drawing of the ancient Market Cross, Chichester.

Distributors:
Australia, New Zealand, South-east Asia:
Jacaranda-Wiley Ltd., Jacaranda Press,
JOHN WILEY & SONS INC.,
G.P.O. Box 859, Brisbane, Queensland 40001, Australia

Canada:
JOHN WILEY & SONS CANADA LIMITED
22 Worcester Road, Rexdale, Ontario, Canada.

Europe, Africa:
JOHN WILEY & SONS LIMITED
Baffins Lane, Chichester, West Sussex, England.

North and South America and the rest of the world:
Halsted Press: a division of
JOHN WILEY & SONS
605 Third Avenue, New York, N.Y. 10016, U.S.A.

© 1984 M. Wallace/Ellis Horwood Limited

British Library Cataloguing in Publication Data
Wallace, Mark
Communicating with databases in natural language. —
(Ellis Horwood series in artificial intelligence)
1. Prolog (Computer program language)
I. Title
001.64'24   QA76.73.P7

Library of Congress Card No.

ISBN 0-85312-639-9 (Ellis Horwood Limited)
ISBN 0-470-20105-3 (Halsted Press)

Typeset by Ellis Horwood Limited
Printed in Great Britain by R.J. Acford, Chichester

COPYRIGHT NOTICE —
All Rights Reserved. No part of this publication may be reproduced, stored in a retrieval system, or transmitted, in any form or by any means, electronic, mechanical, photocopying, recording or otherwise, without the permission of Ellis Horwood Limited, Market Cross House, Cooper Street, Chichester, West Sussex, England.

Table of Contents

Preface 9

Chapter 1 INTRODUCTION
1. Natural language processing 11
2. Communicating with databases 12
3. Making query languages more habitable 14
4. NL system architecture 15
5. The scope of the implementation 16

Chapter 2 NATURAL LANGUAGE ENQUIRY
1. Introduction 17
2. The parser 21
3. Extensibility of the grammar 27
4. The English dictionary 29
5. Spelling correction 32
6. Context 33
7. The data model 38
8. Query language 40
9. DBMS independence 43
10. Topic independence 43
11. Pragmatics 44

12. General queries 47
13. Referring back to the user 48
14. QPROC 48

Chapter 3 FORMALISING NATURAL LANGUAGE
1. The difference between natural language and formal languages 50
2. QPROC objectives 51

Chapter 4 D&QS
1. Arriving at D&Qs 56
2. Semantic concepts 66
3. Converting D&Qs to simplified RDBMS 'List Commands' 71

Chapter 5 SEMANTICS
1. Introduction 82
2. The sentence, or clause 84
3. Data modelling 94
4. Noun phrases 97
5. The verb "to be" 106

Chapter 6 IMPLEMENTATION
1. Introduction 108
2. Functionality 108
3. QPROC design 113

Chapter 7 CURRENT DEVELOPMENTS IN NATURAL LANGUAGE ACCESS TO DATABASES
1. Introduction 121
2. Current systems 121
3. Mapping natural language onto current databases 122
4. Developments 124
5. Networking 126

Appendix 1 A PILOT IMPLEMENTATION 128

Appendix 2 SPECIFICATION OF D&QS 133

Appendix 3   A PROLOG PROGRAM FOR CONVERTING D&QS TO LIST COMMANDS   143

Appendix 4   THE ELECTION AND COPSE DATABASES   150

Appendix 5   INTRODUCTION TO PROLOG   156

References   163

Index   167

To Jan and Ian

Preface

This book is intended to give the reader an insight into the construction of a natural language front end.

The first chapter introduces natural language systems in general, but the remainder of the book concentrates on natural language (NL) front ends to databases. The second chapter attempts to bring out the essential issues by examining a variety of solutions implemented in existing NL front ends. The next four chapters focus in on a particular implementation, QPROC, in order to give the reader the more detailed understanding that cannot be gleaned from general surveys. In Chapter 4 it is presumed that the reader has some knowledge of logic, although all the logical constructs are fully illustrated with examples. In Chapter 5 QPROC's NL analysis is described but the linguistic concepts are introduced in non-technical terms. A section on data modelling assumes that the reader has some prior knowledge of the relational data model.

The last two chapters contain practical discussion — in Chapter 6 about the implementation of QPROC, in Chapter 7 about the current status and near term developments of NL front ends.

The whole book is spiced with examples of PROLOG programming to illustrate the implementation of QPROC and the suitability of PROLOG for the task. The book does not claim to be an introduction to PROLOG, but there is an appendix designed to bring the reader to a point where he can understand the example PROLOG programs, if such a text is not available to him.

That the book appeared at all can be traced back to Terry Smith and Roger Pikett of the BBC, and to Professor David Barron of Southampton University and Andrew Hutt of ICL, who agreed to the joint sponsorship of a Ph.D. on a natural language database interface. I am very grateful to the SERC, ICL and the BBC for the funding of three years of research under David Barron's bolstering supervision; to Andrew Hutt who whirled me back to ICL where I have been pointed in the right direction, supported and encouraged by David Horth and Vince West; and to Ken Whitehead and Professor John Campbell who have read the book and who have both shown me a number of improvements which I have included in their entirety.

My initial interest in natural language understanding was sparked off and stoked by Alan Bond, at Queen Mary College, London. Throughout my research I have been continually encouraged and helped by my parents whose confidence in me will never be justified by anything I produce but was inevitably most inspiring!

Finally, to Julie who spent hours decoding my writing, typing and retyping it, I acknowledge a tremendous debt which cannot properly be expressed in this preface.

1

Introduction

1. NATURAL LANGUAGE PROCESSING

Computers never get jokes. In fact they can cope with so few of the functions of natural language that nobody has ever dared claim to have written a real natural language understanding system. What this book describes, and what perhaps one hundred groups of people are working on all over the world, are merely systems to deal with useful subsets of natural language. These groups are interested in natural language for a variety of different reasons. There is a purely research aspect and this is termed 'computational linguistics'. It is closely linked to computer science, linguistics, psychology and philosophy. Research has produced natural language (NL) systems to simulate a psychiatrist, to generate children's stories, to paraphrase and precis, and even to place a political interpretation on a set of facts.

The first practical application of NL was for machine translation from one language to another. At the moment this application is being heavily funded by the European Economic Community to cope with the seven official languages into which every document has to be translated! Currently there is still no machine translation, only machine-*aided* translation — the output of the computer is not a good translation and it needs to be edited by a linguist to make it idiomatic.

Machine translation systems have to cover quite a large vocabulary, without really 'understanding' the meaning of the subject matter. Naively, the system only has to know enough to find which word or phrase in the target language is closest to each word or phrase in the input.

Another area of application is for 'adviser' systems. Such systems need to be given a great deal of knowledge about a specific area so that they can detect the users' errors and explain them. These systems can appear extremely 'intelligent' as long as the conversation sticks closely to the application area. Surprisingly they have almost nothing in common with natural language translation systems, and an expert at programming machine translation systems might have very little idea how to set about building an adviser.

Natural language analysis is also required for automatic extraction of information from text. The information is then recorded in some standard form suitable to be input to a database, or efficiently searched by further software.

More divergent areas of development include natural language generation, so that computers don't have to talk gobbledygook, and processing spoken language, which is still at a rather speculative stage.

Major computer users are currently most interested, however, in natural language modules which fit on top of other computer software. Given the current interest in expert systems, a natural language 'front end' seems a very promising way to provide a man—machine interface to such complex software. In particular, natural language output to express the expert system's 'reasoning' would be very useful.

Many computer systems offer a range of tools for data extraction, statistical analysis and graphical output. Usually the tools have been developed quite independently and the user has to express similar commands to the different software packages in very different ways. A natural language 'front end' to all the different packages would enable the user to forget which package he† was using and how to address it. Thus, users are interested in natural language as a standard man—machine interface.

2. COMMUNICATING WITH DATABASES

The computer software best suited to benefit from a natural language front end is the database. Typically databases hold huge quantities of data which have to be stored in complex ways so as to secure the fastest access for the maximum proportion of queries. Many formal query languages have been designed to simplify the problem of getting the correct data out of this monolith.

These formal languages can be divided into 'one-dimensional' languages — composed of letters, numbers and mathematical signs — and 'two-dimensional' languages which enable the user to manipulate diagrams on a screen. A very good two-dimensional language is Query By Example [61]. An example query is

"List the products ordered by Good Co."

---

† I apologise for having used the third person pronoun in the masculine gender throughout!

(Words in lower case are typed on the screen by the user. The attribute names are generated by the system):

orderline	PRODUCTORDER	ORDER	QUANTITY
	p. <u>product</u>	<u>order</u>	

order	ID	ORDERDATE	CUSTOMER
	<u>order</u>		<u>cust</u>

customer	ID	CUSTNAME	ADDRESS1	ADDRESS2	COUNTY	POSTCODE	...
	<u>cust</u>	good co					

(The database against which this query is being evaluated is the 'COPSE' database of Appendix 4).

"Despite the great practical differences between the many formal languages, linear or two-dimensional, many of the same criticisms apply to all", writes Cuff [7]. "In each system the user must form a query using not only a description of the data, but also a set of artificial syntactic, constructional and navigational elements to encase it."

Another problem is the requirement for completeness in a formal query language which unnecessarily complicates the definition of the language for casual users. Cuff writes, "Why emphasise a full syntax and precedence rules for combining logical operators, when they avoid complex queries and mishandle formal logic? ... If some extra syntax is mandatory in order to eliminate ambiguity in certain infrequent cases, then it may be better to remove it ... The ambiguity can be resolved by explaining the choices to the user when it arises".

Thirdly, a query formulation may be objectively much more complex than one would expect from the corresponding English question. For example in Query By Example, the query "List the products held at Bracknell" (against the COPSE database) is:

stock	PRODUCTSTOCK	STOCKWHSE	BINID	QTYONHAND	...
	p. <u>product</u>	bracknell			

while the previous example, "List the products ordered by Good Co." sounds no more complicated but requires three different tables.

Another pair of examples of queries expressed similarly in English but not (yet) in formal languages, is "What costs more than £50?" and "What costs more than desks?".

3. MAKING QUERY LANGUAGES MORE HABITABLE

Many of the shortcomings of formal query languages can be overcome by extending them and giving more intelligence to the interpreter.

By doing less with syntax and more with word meanings, the language can reduce the necessity for the user to conform to an artificial syntax. If the formal words have a meaning close to their natural meaning, the burden on the user is further reduced, especially if all alternative natural language words with the same meaning are allowable synonyms in the formal language. A final refinement would be to make the remaining syntax correspond to the syntax of natural language.

A second improvement would be to reduce the requirement for the user to know about the details of the database. Natural language synonyms for all database names are an obvious start, but also the facility for the interpreter to navigate around the database would be a great advantage (e.g. enabling the two Query By Example queries to be phrased in a similar way). The ability to use the structure of the data as well as the structure of the query to aid the interpretation of the user's input will be further discussed in the next chapter.

A third improvement that would be possible with an intelligent interpreter is to recognise the user's intended query on the basis of incomplete or slightly erroneous input. Thus simple queries could be recognised in a very abbreviated form (e.g. "Age Smith") although more complex queries such as "Which salesman had at least two customers ordering desks in June?" may need more complete expression. Queries with minor syntactic errors could be recognised if the remainder of the query was sufficiently unambiguous.

Another improvement would be to enable the user to phrase his queries incrementally. Thus his original query might be ambiguous and the system could prompt him to select which interpretation he intended. Or else the user could phrase a simple query ("How many customers are in debit?") and follow it up with supplementaries ("And who are they?").

Finally, an intelligent interpreter could perhaps recognise logical inconsistencies in a query and warn the user, or answer a broader but consistent query (e.g. "List orders placed by Good Co. and Better Co" could be interpreted as "List orders placed by either Good Co. or Better Co.").

Finally, two other desirable features of a query language are *curtness* and *breadth of use*.

Clearly all these are facilities which 'natural language front ends' are aiming to provide. In particular natural language is powerful and precise where required, but also curt, and it does provide a conversational interface which enables the user to ask incremental queries.

The description 'natural language' may be a drawback because it suggests capabilities beyond any current or foreseeable implementation. It tempts the user to ask common sense questions outside the area of the database's body of information, or evaluative questions within it. Tennant found that users tended to try a range of interactions outside the realm of database enquiry when provided with an NL interface [45].

The term 'natural language' front end is used for a good reason, however. It implies that the user should not consciously have to translate his queries into terms appropriate for the front end. Language users do unconsciously adapt their way of speaking to their audience, however, and the natural language subset accepted by the NL front end should be 'dense' enough for the user to click into it without conscious effort.

As long as a user does not have a vastly over-optimistic expectation of what the system can do for him, the intelligent natural language database front end can enable him to get the right answers with less frustration, and little requirement for technical support.

4. NL SYSTEM ARCHITECTURE

The modules of an NL database front end are

— the parser
— the formal query generator
— the database access routines.

It is not sensible, however, for the system first to perform a parse, then to construct a query and then to access the data. The grammatical analysis of a sentence is closely dependent upon its meaning, so the grammar must be tailored to the system's knowledge structure. With the development of data modelling and the implementation of data dictionaries it has become possible automatically to tailor the parser to a particular application by writing into the parser calls on the data dictionary.

Thus the parser uses the same information as the query generator and so formal queries can be built up during the parse. In fact, if a formal query cannot be built up from the input sentence, the parse fails. This places a burden on the formal query language. It must be powerful enough to express even queries which, for implementational reasons, cannot be executed against the data. A further requirement is for the formal queries to yield sensible answers. Thus "Is the Tory candidate at Worthing over 50?" should get a more sensible answer than "no" if there is no Tory candidate at Worthing. In fact the QPROC system described in this book actually evaluates the formal interpretation of definite noun phrases (like "the Tory candidate at Worthing") against the database before completing the parse of the input query.

It follows that the formal language in the QPROC system is the fulcrum on which the parser and database access routines are pivoted. The discussion of the parser is to a considerable degree expressed in terms of the formal subqueries generated by the different grammatical constructions.

Another fundamental feature of the design of an NL database front end is application independence. There is a trade-off between the size of the NL subset the system covers, and its adaptability to new databases. An NL interface *builder* is a system whose grammar and formal query generator must be completely rewritten for each new application. Such a system provides useful tools for constructing these components. The tools used have a major impact on the character of the generated system. LIFER [22] is an NL interface builder, and the systems it generates are very impressive.

Other systems provide considerable adaptability without any rewriting of the parser. A very good example is TEAM [19] which includes an 'acquisition component', enabling a database expert to tailor the system to a new application by simply answering questions about the structure and meaning of items in the database.

The QPROC system is more similar to TEAM, though considerably less comprehensive.

5. THE SCOPE OF THE IMPLEMENTATION

J. L. Austin roughly divided sentences into five categories:

(1) Objective judgements
(2) Ordering, advising, questioning
(3) Promising, understanding
(4) Social behaviour — apologising, congratulating
(5) Taking a stance — replying, assuming, conceding.

Of all these, an NL database front end can only deal with a small proportion of judgements, orders and questions. There is considerable research on the analysis of speech acts which throws further light on (2) and (5), but this will not be dealt with in the discussion of the current implementation.

Another research topic may be termed 'knowledge representation'. Firstly this encompasses the structure required to express facts, opinions, etc., and secondly it must include work on the objects of knowledge. Thus, for example, if disparate statements are to be interpreted as giving knowledge about the same thing, then the research must investigate the common primitive concepts underlying the different phrasings. In this book the 'knowledge representation' is simply the database and data 'model', and only current database concepts are used.

NL front ends, then, have the limited objective of coping with as 'habitable' as possible a natural language subset, given the available data modelling concepts. The design is, in a sense, bottom-up, starting with the data model, superimposing as powerful as possible a query language, and then using linguistic tools to map natural language sentences onto formal language.

2

Natural language enquiry

1. INTRODUCTION

Until a few years ago, it was possible to survey all existing natural language understanding systems in one paper [54]. A 1982 questionnaire [25], however, yielded over one hundred summaries of natural language understanding systems, including a considerable proportion with a database access component. In order to provide a framework for this chapter we will, therefore, dissect natural language database enquiry into a set of relatively independent subparts, and survey the best approaches to each.

The most fundamental concept in designing a natural language system is the interface between natural language understanding and database query. We first examine the scope of such an interface in general terms. The interface imposes two kinds of restriction upon the natural language understanding (NLU) module. The first kind of restriction is 'informational'. The NLU can only understand words referring to the subject area covered by the database, e.g. personnel information for a company, or geological information for an area. Thus an NLU attached to a geological database would understand the word "lime" in the geological sense, but not as a type of fruit.

The second kind of restriction is 'structural'. Structural restrictions are due to the data structures in the database. For example, a text database would impose quite different structural restrictions from a relational database. A database of flat files would impose different restrictions from a Codasyl database. The structural restrictions limit the possible interpretations of a natural language query to only those which can be represented in the data model.

1.1 An example of structural restrictions

The English language includes two kinds of words, *content* words, which mean something on their own, and *function* words, which gain their meaning from other words in the sentences in which they occur. The word "than" is a function word which is meaningful in comparative contexts: "I did better *than* you did". If a data model comprises "entities" and "properties" then every content word must map onto an 'entity' or a 'property'. A function word is just part of a phrase (or clause) in a sentence. Each such phrase (or clause) maps onto some construction in a formal query language which can be used to query the data. Such a query language might include the construct:

PRINT ⟨property name⟩ OF ⟨entity value⟩

e.g.

"PRINT AGE OF EMP:ROBERT".

(We shall use "⟨", "⟩" throughout to indicate that the word enclosed names a whole class of items which may occur in this position.)

We could represent (one use of) the word "is" by the pattern

"What ⟨noun phrase 1⟩ is ⟨noun phrase 2⟩?"

e.g. "What age is Robert?".

"PRINT AGE OF EMP:ROBERT"

is the formal query which represents the meaning of "What age is Robert?".

The statement can be generalised to say:

If "X" is the meaning of NP1 (= noun phrase 1)
and "Y" is the meaning of NP2
then "PRINT X OF Y" is the meaning of "What ⟨NP1⟩ is ⟨NP2⟩?"

The example shows that the meaning of a phrase (or clause) containing a function word is generally dependent on the meaning of the content words in that phrase (or clause).

The example also shows how the traditional grammatical categories (such as 'noun phrase') are seldom precise enough to yield a unique meaning for database enquiry. Thus the same pattern — "What ⟨NP1⟩ is ⟨NP2⟩?" — would also match "What item is £50?" although "item" is very unlikely to be represented in any entity/property database as a 'property'.

1.2 Informational restrictions

We have, albeit briefly, discussed how the structural restrictions impinge on the NLU. The informational restrictions can, quite simply, confine the NLU to knowledge contained in the database by recognising only those words in the English dictionary which pertain to the data. Thus an NLU attached to a personnel database which had no information about families might be asked "Who is

Smith's father?". The NLU's response, at best, can only be "The database has no information about employees' families".

(In fact, the way current NLU-database interfaces work, the English dictionary for the *NLU* only contains words that pertain to the *data*. The actual response to the "Smith's father" question in current systems would be: "The word 'Father' is not recognised".)

1.3 "Applicability" restrictions

Some attempt has been made to distinguish informational and structural restrictions because databases with the same structure can contain information on totally different subjects, and databases with different structures may contain information on the same topic. When, however, an NLU is attached to a particular database, the informational and structural restrictions combine to yield tighter restrictions than the sum of both.

We have seen how the English query,

"What age is Robert?"

matches the pattern,

What ⟨NP1⟩ is ⟨NP2⟩?

which maps onto,

PRINT X OF Y

where X is the meaning of "age", and Y is the meaning of "Robert".
The structural restrictions are:

(1) That the first noun phrase, NP1, maps onto a 'property'
(2) That the second noun phrase, NP2, maps onto an 'entity'
(3) That the sentence "What ⟨NP1⟩ is ⟨NP2⟩?" is properly represented by the formal query "PRINT ⟨property name⟩ OF ⟨entity value⟩".

The informational restrictions are:

(1) That "age" has meaning "X"
(2) That "Robert" has meaning "Y".

Consider the question "What price is Robert?". This question appears meaningless (and indeed it may be), but let us suppose that the database contains information, not just about employees and their ages, but also about *toys* and their prices. Now "What price is Robert (the employee)?" is meaningless, and the formal query

PRINT PRICE OF EMP:ROBERT

will fail.

Perhaps, though, there is a toy robot called "Robert", and the question "What price is Robert" is supposed to yield the formal query

PRINT PRICE OF TOY:ROBERT

The NLU—database interface can select the correct meaning of this query through knowledge of *how* the information is stored in the structure of the database. This produces a new set of restrictions which will only allow queries such as "What ⟨NP1⟩ is ⟨NP2⟩?" if the property denoted by NP1 is *applicable* to the entity denoted by NP2. Thus the first meaning, "EMP:ROBERT", of "Robert" fails to meet the new restrictions, and is rejected in favour of the second meaning, "TOY:ROBERT".

These restrictions are called 'applicability' restrictions and they can be of considerable use in removing ambiguity from English sentences. A typical example of ambiguity in English is when qualifying phrases occur together:

"The flower *in the vase which stood on the mantelpiece* ..."

"The shop *in the high street which sells flowers* ...".

The second qualifying phrase may qualify either the immediately preceding noun ("the vase which stood on the mantelpiece"), or the first noun ("the shop ... which sells flowers"). People who speak English do not perceive ambiguity in either sentence. Clearly "the flower ... which stood on the mantelpiece" does not make sense, and nor does "... the high street which sells flowers". Instead of extending the NLU's grammar somehow so as to preclude the ambiguity, it saves duplication of effort to allow the applicability restrictions to remove it.

1.4 Modules in natural language enquiry systems

Having explored, in a very general way, the requirements for putting a natural language "front end" on a database, we will now look in more detail at various modules within existing such systems and their implementation in currently working programs. We will investigate:

— The parser
— Extensibility of the grammar
— The English dictionary
— Spelling correction
— Context
— The data model
— Query language
— DBMS independence
— Topic independence
— Pragmatics
— General queries
— Referring back to the user

2. THE PARSER

The "parser" is the program that analyses the grammar of a sentence. English grammar provides the relevant context for understanding each *function* word in the English language (see section 1.1 above). In the example

"What age is Robert and what is his salary?"

the grammatical analysis yield two clauses, the first of which, "What age is Robert . . .", provides the context for the function word "is". There is not a sharp distinction between function words and content words, and a content word such as "horse" can also have different meanings in different contexts like a function word. "Horse" can be a noun, as in "How fast is that horse?"; but it can also be a *classifier,* as in *"horse* fly". A horse fly is not, of course, a type of horse but a type of fly.

English grammar, then, defines the function of each word in an English sentence.

2.1 LIFER

From the descriptions of some currently implemented parsers it is very hard to tell what grammars they analyse. The LIFER system [22] is, however, exceptionally comprehensible. Thus to include the sentence

"What ⟨noun-phrase1⟩ is ⟨noun-phrase2⟩?"

in the grammar, the LIFER parser simply requires a 'production':

SENTENCE → WHAT ⟨NP1⟩ IS ⟨NP2⟩ | 'print *NP1* of *NP2*'

"NP1" and "NP2" are 'non-terminals', which have their own productions†. The part after the vertical bar, 'print *NP1* of *NP2*', is the meaning of the sentence, where *NP1* is the meaning of noun-phrase1 and *NP2* is the meaning of noun-phrase2.

In general the semantic part (i.e. the part after the vertical bar) in a LIFER production can be any expression that returns the meaning. This expression may be used to augment the grammar, since it can return the value *ERROR* which causes the parser to reject the production. The augmentation could be used to implement the applicability restrictions of section 1.3 above. Thus for

SENTENCE → WHAT ⟨NP1⟩ IS ⟨NP2⟩ | expression

the "expression" might be used to check that NP2 referred to an entity, and NP1 referred to a property applicable to that entity.

---

† The actual syntax for defining productions to the LIFER parser is more complicated.

The LIFER parser is a top-down, left-to-right parser. When attempting to match the single production

SENTENCE → WHAT ⟨NP1⟩ IS ⟨NP2⟩ | expression

onto an English sentence, the LIFER parser:

(1) Looks for the word "what"
(2) Looks for a noun-phrase, and extracts its meaning *NP1*
(3) Looks for the word "is"
(4) Looks for another noun-phrase, and extracts its meaning *NP2*
(5) Evaluates the expression.

At any stage the match may fail. Concentrating too much "intelligence" into the expression may cause the parser to do a great deal of matching which ultimately fails because the expression yields the *ERROR* result. In the LIFER grammar for the US Navy's LADDER system therefore, the applicability restrictions are built into the *grammar* rather than the augmentation.

Thus four example productions for SENTENCE are:

SENTENCE → ⟨PRESENT⟩ THE ⟨ATTRIBUTE⟩ OF ⟨SHIP⟩ | e1
          ⟨PRESENT⟩ ⟨SHIP'S⟩ ⟨ATTRIBUTE⟩ | e2
          HOW MANY ⟨SHIP⟩ ARE THERE | e3
          HOW MANY ⟨SHIP⟩ ARE THERE WITH ⟨PROPERTY⟩ | e4.

This grammar has no noun-phrases, or verb-phrases, but rather a special set of categories for the particular task of providing a front end for the LADDER system. To avoid any unnecessary *backtracking* these productions are compiled into a "transition tree" which can be diagrammed as in Fig. 2.1. The clarity of

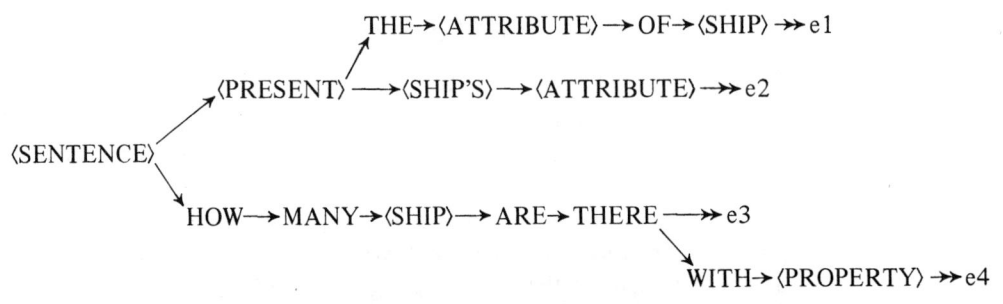

```
                    THE→⟨ATTRIBUTE⟩→OF→⟨SHIP⟩ ↠ e1
                   ↗
         ⟨PRESENT⟩ — → ⟨SHIP'S⟩ → ⟨ATTRIBUTE⟩ ↠ e2
        ↗
⟨SENTENCE⟩
        ↘
         HOW → MANY → ⟨SHIP⟩ → ARE → THERE ──↠ e3
                                            ↘
                                             WITH → ⟨PROPERTY⟩ ↠ e4
```

Fig. 2.1 – A transition tree.

design of the LIFER parser is self-evident. The design also provides for excellent facilities to extend the grammar, a very clever spelling module, the power to deal with short follow-up questions, and a well-defined interface to the database.

2.2 PLANES

LIFER's transition trees are based on a simplification of the 'Augmented Transition Network' ("ATN", [58]). We can redraw the transition tree as a transition network (Fig. 2.2). This network is a "simple" network. It has no cycles, and a

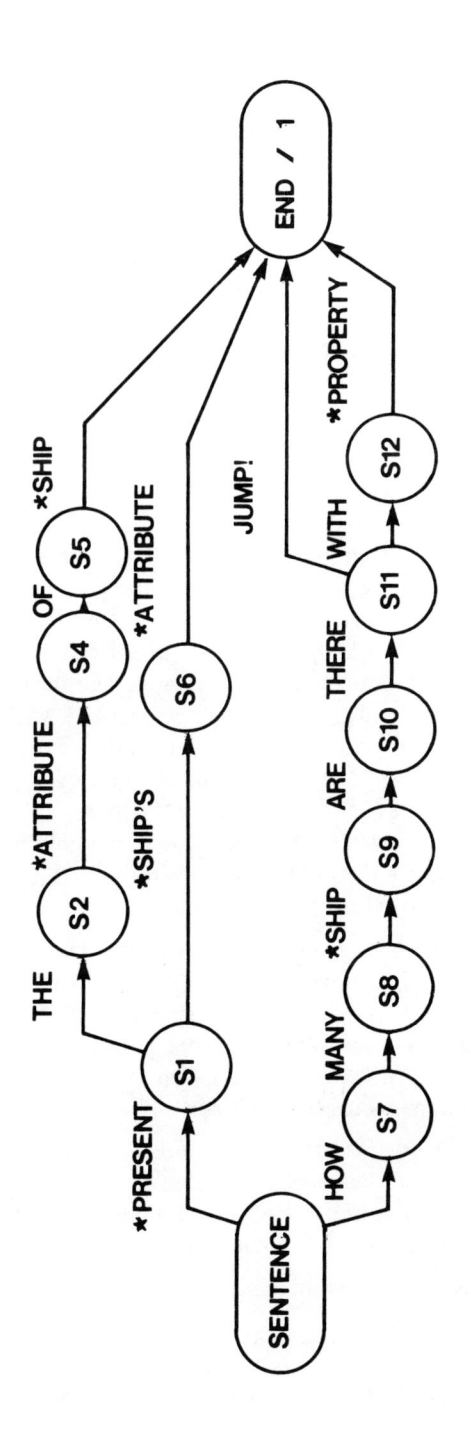

Fig. 2.2 – A transition network.

single start and end node. In fact *any* unaugmented transition network is equivalent to a set of simple networks which, in turn, can be translated into a LIFER transition tree.

An augmented transition network also includes a set of registers which can be set, tested and altered as the parser works its way through the network. When the ATN parser reaches a "subnet" (such as "*SHIP" in the network above), it does three things:

(1) It performs any tests that may be specified by the grammar before entering the subnet.
(2) It passes arguments to the subnet if required (e.g. a verbphrase requires a *number* argument, such as "1st person singular", so as to maintain agreement with the subject; as in "I am", "You are" . . .).
(3) It gets a clean set of registers for use with the subnet.

When an ATN parser exits from a subnet it evaluates a "meaning" expression just as a LIFER parser does.

All this sophistication enables an ATN-based parser, such as PLANES [49], to parse sentences in a very different manner; see Fig. 2.3. This network is not claimed to be precisely that used in the PLANES system, but it illustrates the features of an ATN which can provide the benefits detailed below. In the network each loop simply fills up another register. The meaning of the sentence is then extracted at the end by matching the registers with a template. The template automatically maps the register contents into a formal database query. Thus, for example, the "*ACTION" loop can recognise verb phrases in active or passive form and its result is inserted in the ACTION register. Similarly there are registers for the time period, and for the various possible noun-phrases. This approach yields considerable flexibility in the parser.

Goodman writes of PLANES [16]:

> The central novel assumption underlying the model is that a database request is uniquely determined by the *set* of semantic constituents, independent of their order.
>
> > [e.g. "In 1981 McEnroe won Wimbledon"; "McEnroe won Wimbledon in 1981". Notice, though, that the order in which registers were filled could be recorded if necessary.]
>
> We need only sufficient grammatical correctness to recognise phrase boundaries of semantic constituents and to recognise clause boundaries (if any) . . . Thus the model handles grammatical English, pidgin English, or ungrammatical lists of semantic constituents with equal ease.
>
> > [e.g. "Total maintenance, A7's, 1974"].

To extend PLANES's grammar to cover a new type of sentence just one new template need be added, and then all kinds of variations on the sentence — active and passive forms, ellipsis, different phrase orderings, and noise words — are automatically covered by the grammar.

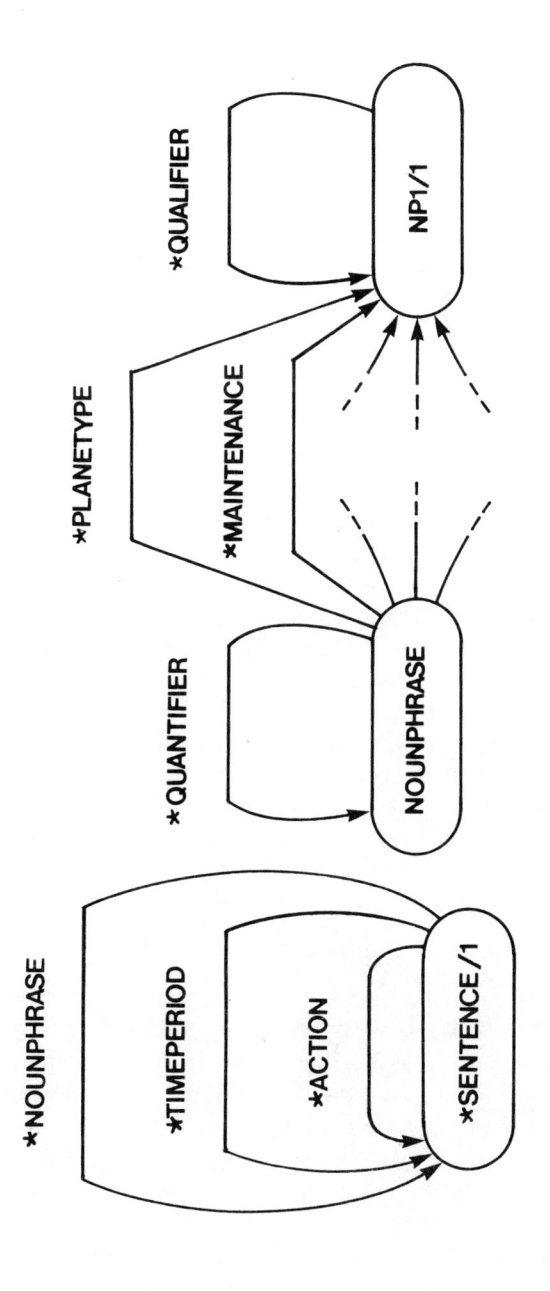

Fig. 2.3 — A network and subnetwork which utilise augmentations.

2.3 Semantic grammar

The PLANES parser includes many subnets, such as "*PLANETYPE", which are oriented towards the information held in the database. A grammar tailored like this to a particular application is called a semantic grammar. LADDER also employs a semantic grammar since it includes non-terminals such as "⟨SHIP⟩". Semantic grammars suffer from a major drawback. They become highly redundant when expanded for more general use because they fail to capture certain generalisations about English as a whole. In fact all grammars for natural language enquiry systems must be semantic grammars because of the informational and structural restrictions imposed by the interface to the data (see section 1 above).

The PLANES system, however, *does* make use of some generalisations about qualifying phrases (e.g. "Qualifiers appear after the main noun in a noun phrase, and are often introduced by relative pronouns such as "which" or "that", or by a verb ending in -*ed*, or -*ing*. Prepositional phrases can also serve as qualifiers" [16]). In fact the qualifier subnet in the PLANES network is "syntax-driven".

This shows that the drawbacks of a semantic grammar can be avoided by retaining in the grammar the categories, such as "noun-phrase" and "verb-phrase" which make available useful generalisations. Only at a lower level need the grammar be tailored to the application.

2.4 REL and INTELLECT

A good example of a system whose grammar retains the generality of English grammar while being adapted for a data model is the REL grammar [46]. The REL grammar differs from LADDER's and PLANES's in that its non-terminals do not reflect the informational restrictions imposed by the application to which REL system is attached. REL does not include categories such as "⟨SHIP⟩", or "*PLANETYPE", but instead it has more general categories such as "name", "relation", "verb table" etc. These categories reflect only the structural restrictions imposed by REL's own data model.

An example of a REL production is

name → ⟨relation⟩ of ⟨name⟩

(e.g. "location of employee" is a 'name', if "location" is a 'relation' and "employee" is a 'name').

The REL data model includes only binary relations, so the relation 'location' is binary. Thus "location of employee" can simply be interpreted as the set of database values linked to each 'employee' via the 'location' relation. Each production for 'name' yields a class of values from the database. If this class is empty then the diagnostic message "VACUOUS DESCRIPTION" is reported to the parser which then tries another parse. Thus REL's grammar is automatically augmented by the applicability restrictions of the database to which it is attached.

INTELLECT [8] is a commercially available system developed from Harris's ROBOT [21]. The INTELLECT grammar is as independent of the application as

REL's, but INTELLECT utilises a data-dictionary to impose informational restrictions upon its grammar.

A problem for domain-independent systems such as REL and INTELLECT is the absence of English *verbs* from databases and data dictionaries. A few verbs, such as "report (on)", "give (me)" are built into INTELLECT, but neither system can derive the meaning of a domain-dependent verb such as "fly" or "sail" from the data model. Moreover such verbs have their own grammar which requires special sophisticated treatment.

The REL solution to the problem is to provide the grammatical framework (Case Analysis [11]) for parsing verbs and to supply only two basic verbs, "to be" and "to have", in the core dictionary. We will see in (section 3.3) how the user is able to define verbs in English.

INTELLECT on the other hand does not distinguish nouns and verbs at all. In fact INTELLECT does not attempt to analyse the English grammar of a query at all – most queries are equally well analysed by INTELLECT if they are reversed!

INTELLECT's grammar is entirely dictated by its applicability restrictions. Consequently "Who sold a car?" and "Who was sold a car?" are indistinguishable to the system. On the other hand there are several advantages to the approach. Firstly, it requires little knowledge of linguistics to set up an application under INTELLECT, and secondly the system performs very well on ill-formed or telegraphic sentences such as "Chicago employees?". Verbs are defined by the knowledge engineer, just like any other words, to map onto a particular data object.

2.5 Other grammars

We have discussed a range of grammars in the context of the restrictions – structural and informational – imposed on each by the interface to the data model. The grammars of LADDER and PLANES are constructed around a particular application, whilst REL supplements a more syntactic grammar with advice from the data dictionary and database.

Other grammars have been written which are supported by a more sophisticated semantics such as preference semantics [52] or conceptual dependency [39]. Although a pilot database enquiry system has been constructed using preference semantics (the Bari system [27]), these two theories are really not aimed at solving problems which are germane to database enquiry.

3. EXTENSIBILITY OF THE GRAMMAR

It is very useful if the grammar for an NLU can be easily extended. This enables the NLU to be adapted to particular dialects or the shorthands of individual users. It also enables the NLU to be updated when the information held in the database is extended. Finally it can provide for those natural language phrases that may just have been missed out in the original grammar.

3.1 NETEDI

The PLANES system has a powerful, and well documented, "network editor" called NETEDI [20]. NETEDI can take new sentence forms, which are rather like productions in LIFER, and automatically weld them into the ATN parser. NETEDI does, however, presume that the user knows about the grammar which is being extended. LIFER and REL can accept grammar extensions from users who are "neither linguists nor logicians" and who must therefore be able to add new definitions and paraphrases in terms of the system's previous English subset.

3.2 LIFER's paraphrase mechanism

The neat design of LIFER's parser enables LIFER to deal with paraphrases in a very powerful way. Suppose, for example, LIFER is told to accept

"For Santa Inez give me the length"

as a paraphrase for

"What is the length of the Santa Inez?"

LIFER will add more than the one sentence "For Santa Inez give me the length" to its grammar. It will also add

"For oilers give me the draft"
"For Kitty Hawk class ships give me the location and commander".

In fact the grammar is extended to include a new *production:*

SENTENCE → FOR ⟨SHIP⟩ GIVE ME THE ⟨ATTRIBUTE⟩ | e1.

The expression, "e1", is elicited from the meaning of the "model" sentence:

"What is the length of the Santa Inez?"

The reason "Santa Inez" can be generalised to "⟨SHIP⟩", and "length" can be generalised to "⟨ATTRIBUTE⟩" in the paraphrase is that each has a match in the model sentence. Thus one paraphrase can extend the grammar to include a large number of new sentences.

One problem with allowing linguistically naive users to extend the grammar is that gaps appear in its coverage: the new grammar may accept one sentence but not another, although they are phrased in a similar way.

3.3 REL definitions

The REL system accepts paraphrases not just for sentences, but for any grammatical category [46]. The same generalisation facility is again employed for any defined word that is written in quotes.

e.g. DEF: MOST EMPTY "SHIP":

"SHIP" WHOSE NET CAPACITY IS THE MAXIMUM NET CAPACITY OF "SHIP"s.

REL also includes the facility to define *verbs*. REL's grammar is a "Case" grammar (see below, Chapter 5 section 2.3), so that, once the 'cases' for a verb are known, the whole variety of possible clauses which use the verb can be accepted by the grammar. Here is an example of a REL verb definition:

> VERB: SHIPS "SAIL" FROM PORTLAND TO VANCOUVER:
> THE PORT OF DEPARTURE OF SHIPS IS PORTLAND
> AND THE DESTINATION OF SHIPS IS VANCOUVER.

This definition establishes the 'cases' for the verb "to sail". It enables REL to parse such sentences as,

> "How many ships sail to Los Angeles from each port?"
> "Which is the most empty ship that sails to Honolulu?"

Unfortunately, no universal set of cases has yet been discovered, so this particular technique may not be equally applicable to all types of information. For the paraphrase of the example the new grammar would not accept the queries:

> "Who sailed ..." (a human subject)
> "Which ship sailed *on May 30th* ..." (a temporal clause)
> "Did Marn sail *out of Portland* ..." (port of departure introduced by a different preposition).

We conclude that some very clever extensibility features have been designed, but for any such feature its effectiveness is heavily dependent on the design of the original core grammar.

4. THE ENGLISH DICTIONARY

4.1 The function of a dictionary

One important function of an English dictionary is to record the correspondences between English words. Consider the dictionary definition of a bachelor, "unmarried man". Suppose, for example, that word-meanings are expressed as relational formulae. Thus the noun "man" means

> $X.man(X)$ (where "X" is a variable, and "*man*" a relation).

The adjective "married" simply means the relation '*married*', and the prefix "un-" means the logical negation "*not*". For the definition of "bachelor" we would like to extract the compound meaning:

> $X. (man(X)\ \&\ not\ married(X))$

from the words "unmarried man".

Similarly the grammar is a kind of dictionary of function words. The production:

> SENTENCE → WHAT ⟨ATTRIBUTE⟩ IS ⟨ENTITY⟩ | PRINT *ATTRIBUTE* OF *ENTITY*

gives the meaning of the words "what" and "is" in the context of this sentence. Moreover definitions can be viewed as extensions to the grammar, so that all verbs, in REL, are defined by the grammar. In a LIFER system even content words can be represented by productions:

   ATTRIBUTE → COUNTRY | ?'NATION
         English word Database name

Extracting the meaning of a word, then is much like extracting the meaning of any grammatical construction in an English sentence. In practice, however, implementing an English dictionary in an NLU is very different from implementing a parser. The vital distinction is that there is a fixed, quite small, number of grammatical categories but a possibly huge number of individual words. Matters of efficiency are of paramount importance in dictionary lookup.

If the grammar of a LIFER NLU included the two productions:

   SENTENCE → WHAT ⟨SHIP⟩ ARE THERE | e1
   SENTENCE → WHAT IS THE ⟨ATTRIBUTE⟩ OF ⟨SHIP⟩ | e2

LIFER would inefficiently try to process the sentence

   "What is the length of the Nautilus?"

by trying to find a ship called "Is". It is a drawback of the top-down approach that this kind of inefficiency creeps more and more into the system as the parser is extended.

One solution is to perform dictionary lookup "bottom-up" — unguided by the parser. This solution also allows the dictionary to be stored in a more traditional fashion: since the dictionary need not be divided into separate sections for each distinct grammatical category, the dictionary can be kept in alphabetical order, and all alternative meanings for each word can be kept together. The bottom-up approach involves inefficiencies of its own, since the system may search blindly for a word when a top-down analysis could guide the search. Thus INTELLECT engages in the following dialogue:

User: CHICAGO IS WHICH EMPLOYEES' CITY?
INTELLECT: IM NOT FAMILIAR WITH THE WORD "CHICAGO".
      IF ITS A WORD YOU EXPECT TO FIND IN THE DATABASE
      HIT THE RETURN KEY. OTHERWISE EITHER FIX ITS
      SPELLING OR ENTER A SYNONYM FOR IT.
User: [return]
INTELLECT: WHAT FIELD SHOULD IT APPEAR IN?
User: city
    ...

With the top-down knowledge that the next word should describe a city, the system could look through the list of cities in the database and avoid the necessity to consult the user.

A further question is whether to search for alternative meanings for a given word. The INTELLECT system cannot, for example, deal with a word that has one "familiar" meaning, and is also a database value. The question of "how hard to try" will also come up in the context of spelling correction; (see section 5).

4.2 Semantics

In our discussion of meaning we are confined to the data models implemented in currently working databases. A word can therefore name a relation (or record), an attribute (or field), a segment (or set) or a database value. The defined words have meanings which are constructed out of the above.

Three basic concepts of semantics are synonymy, incompatibility and hyponymy. Two synonyms are simply words which mean the same. Incompatibles are words which exclude each other (such as "married" and "single"). A hyponym is a word whose meaning is subordinate to the meaning of another word, so "employee" is a hyponym of "person".

In terms of our data models we can illustrate synonymy and incompatibility quite straightforwardly. Two synonyms refer to the same value in the database, and two incompatibles to *alternative* values. Incompatibles are useful for distinguishing the "conjunctive" use of the English word "and" ("John is tall *and* thin"), and the "disjunctive" use ("List employees named Lawler *and* Smith"). The *disjunctive* use of "and" only occurs when it joins incompatibles. NLUs that can deal with these uses of "and" are the system defined by M. King in [27], INTELLECT and those systems which reject null queries, such as REL.

Hyponymy is a surprisingly important concept for database query because English includes several words like "who" and "when" which can only be mapped onto databases via hyponyms ("who" — "which employee", "which client"; "when" — "what date", "what time"). The really sophisticated approach to hyponymy is the 'subordinate' link in a semantic net [32]. A technique employed with an ordinary relational model is the use of domain hierarchies [10]. In a relational database the database values are divided into a number of separate domains. If "employee" is a domain name, an NLU attached to the database will translate the English word "employee" into a variable, X, that may range over the domain of employees. If a domain hierarchy is implemented which includes

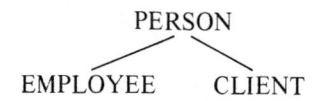

```
            PERSON
           /      \
      EMPLOYEE   CLIENT
```

then the English word "person" translates into a variable which may range over employees or clients. (Domain hierarchies are also mentioned in Chapter 5, section 3.2).

One other semantic concept is antonymy, where two words contrast with each other. Examples are "large" and "small", "high" and "low". Such words are not mutually exclusive since, for example, a large mouse is a small animal.

32   NATURAL LANGUAGE ENQUIRY   [Ch.

Thus sentences which use antonyms are only true to a degree. To deal with such language a fuzzy logic system such as PRUF [60] would be required, but this is well beyond current data model implementations. Notice that NLUs can deal with queries such as "how high . . .", if the database stores heights as numeric values. In this case, comparisons can also be dealt with such as "higher than" and "lower than".

5. SPELLING CORRECTION

When INTELLECT fails to recognise an English word it enters into a dialogue with the user such as the example in the last section. Two systems that attempt to guess the misspelt word before resorting to a dialogue with the user are PLANES and LIFER.

5.1 Detection of spelling errors

Firstly, there are bound to be some spelling mistakes that will not even be spotted by the spelling corrector. If dictionary lookup is bottom-up, as in PLANES, then a misspelling that yields another word (e.g. "plan" for "plane"), will not be detected. On the other hand if dictionary lookup is top-down then spelling errors will be indistinguishable from grammatical errors, because the system will only be able to record that no word *of the right category* could be found. This is the situation in the LIFER system. Faced with a misspelling (or a grammar error), LIFER fails the parse and tries a different production, recording at which point in the sentence the failure occurs. If the sentence cannot be parsed LIFER treats its rightmost failpoint as a spelling error, and tries spelling correction.

5.2 Correcting spelling errors

Given that a system detects a misspelt word, the word is matched against a list of correct words. If any of these are a good enough match, the system confirms the spelling correction with the user, and the sentence is parsed with the new word. (LIFER does not check back with the user until the parse is complete.)

To ensure the spelling correction is fast and efficient, the list of alternatives must be kept as short as possible, and the matching algorithm must be as fast as possible.

List of alternatives.   Clearly a top-down dictionary-lookup will ensure that the list of alternatives is as short as possible. Furthermore it would be sensible to confine spelling correction to the *core* dictionary, so as to avoid extensive searching through the data dictionary or database.

Matching algorithm.   One matching algorithm looks for single letter substitutions, insertion or removal of a single letter, or reversal of two letters. This algorithm involves performing the reverse operation on the misspelt word and looking for a match. The PLANES system, however, uses a kind of template matching which gives a score for each match. The word which matches best is suggested as the correct spelling. A fuller discussion of possible matching algorithms is in [49].

6. CONTEXT

So far we have seen how an NLU processes sentences in isolation. There are a number of English constructions, however, which allow sentences to refer to previous questions and answers, and to various other things (such as today's date) which are meaningful only in context. *Anaphora* is the device of making in a sentence a reference which can only be interpreted in the current context (for definitions and a full discussion see Hirst [23]).

The components of the context must include:

(1) Preset values.
(2) Words, phrases and clauses which have recently occurred in the discourse.
(3) The meanings of such words, phrase and clauses.
(4) Things previously referred to during the discourse.

"Preset values" refer to the current time, date and perhaps location and user name. They also include any default values introduced explicitly or implicitly into the discourse (e.g. "From now on only consider A7s" [16, page 61]).

The discussion of working implementations will focus on three types of anaphor:

(1) Substitutes and ellipsis.
(2) Definite noun-phrases.
(3) Pronominal reference.

In the first type, (1), the NLU merely has to substitute the meaning of some previous word, phrase or clause for the anaphor. In the second type the system needs to cut down the class of things which could be referred to by the noun-phrase so as to yield only *the* ones intended by the definite noun-phrase. This may involve two possible components of the context — preset values and things previously referred to. The third type of anaphor, pronominal reference, generally refers back to something previously referred to. However, the problem of deciding *which* thing is extraordinarily difficult.

6.1 Substitutes and ellipsis

6.1.1 LUNAR

Woods's LUNAR system [59] can deal with substitutes such as the following:

"Give me *all analyses of sample 10046* for hydrogen.
Give me *them* for oxygen."

In the second sentence the pronoun, "them", stands for "all analyses of sample 10046". To find a match for "them", LUNAR searches through antecedent noun-phrases for one with a parallel syntactic and semantic structure.

For every grammatical structure that may be subsequently referred to anaphorically LUNAR enters its 'meaning' into the context. Thus the 'meaning' of "all analyses of sample 10046" is available as the 'meaning' of "them" in the second sentence.

LUNAR's semantics also enables it to deal with the following:

"What is the silicon content *of each volcanic sample?*"

"What is *its* magnesium concentration?"

This illustrates LUNAR's ability to cope with quantification and anaphora. A full discussion of this problem is in Webber [51].

One problem with LUNAR's treatment of anaphoric reference in general is that only the phrases typed in by the user in previous questions are available for anaphoric reference.

6.1.2 SHRDLU

Winograd's SHRDLU [56], on the other hand, can search for the referent of a substitute in a previous reply, or even earlier in the same sentence. SHRDLU's heuristic for determining the referent of a substitute is very simple:

(1) Look for a noun-phrase which contrasts with the substitute (e.g. "the green block supports a *big* blue pyramid and a *little* one"). In this case the meaning of the referent is changed to accommodate the new adjective ("little blue pyramid").
(2) If no contrasts can be found just substitute the most recent noun-phrase that contains a head noun.

6.1.3 PLANES

Ellipsis is a kind of substitution where there is not even a word to indicate that something whould be inserted from the context:

"Which *A7s* logged 20 flight hours?"
"Which *ones* logged between 10 and 20 flight hours?" (Substitution)
"Which logged less than 10 flight hours?" (Ellipsis)

PLANES can only deal with substitution and ellipsis when whole phrases (except perhaps the question word in a noun-phrase) are substituted or missed out.

PLANES parses a sentence by filling up a set of registers, each associated with some phrase in the sentence, and then matching the register contents against a "concept case frame". If one or more of the mandatory slots are not filled in then PLANES deduces that substitution or ellipsis is taking place. Thus the PLANES system can detect ellipsis even when there are no clues in the syntactic structure of the sentence.

6.1.4 LIFER

The LIFER system assumes that some ellipsis is taking place when it cannot parse a query. Given the two queries:

"What is the length of the Santa Inez?"
"Displacement?"

LIFER recognises the second query as an abbreviation for

"What is the displacement of the Santa Inez?"

To deal with ellipsis, LIFER picks up from the context the parse tree of the previous input. If the previous sentence contains a substring whose grammatical structure matches the abbreviated query, ("length" → ⟨ATTRIBUTE⟩, "displacement" → ⟨ATTRIBUTE⟩), the new structure is inserted into the old parse tree. This eventually yields a new meaning for the query. The modified parse tree is then available for another elliptical query in case two such queries succeed each other. One question can thus provide the basic pattern for a sequence of short queries:

"What is the length of the Santa Inez?"
"Of the Kennedy"
   (= What is the length of the Kennedy)
"Print the nationality"
   (= Print the nationality of the Kennedy)
"Home ports of American carriers"
   (= Print the home ports of American carriers)

LIFER's ellipsis can only use the previous query as a pattern however. To allow for ellipsis within a sentence (e.g. "What ships are in the Atlantic and what in the Med?") a special production would have to be added for each pattern (e.g. SENTENCE → WHAT ⟨SHIP⟩ ARE ⟨PREDICATE1⟩ AND WHAT ⟨PREDICATE2⟩).

6.2 Definite noun-phrases

6.2.1 Previous referents

Some definite noun-phrases, such as "the Queen of England", refer uniquely and do not require a context. Most definite noun-phrases, however, only refer uniquely when taken in context.

In SHRDLU a definite noun-phrase like "the three red blocks" is evaluated in two stages. First all items are found which fit the description "red blocks". If there are too many (>3) red blocks then SHRDLU checks which three were mentioned most recently, and selects those.

This approach requires that all items ('assertions' in SHRDLU's database) are marked whenever they are used in interpreting or answering a question. Each is marked with the current sentence number so the system will be able to distinguish the most recently mentioned ones. Thus SHRDLU can deal with the following dialogue:

> "What is in the box?"
> "A block and a pyramid."
> "What is behind it?"
> "A red block and another box."
> "What colour is the box?"
> "Green."
> "Pick up *the two blocks*."

6.2.2 Reference relations

But not all definite noun-phrases refer back to things that have been explicitly mentioned before. Consider:

> "Where was the election?"
> "Worthing"
> "Who was *the Conservative candidate*?"

Clearly the last query refers to "The Conservative candidate *in the election*". The missed out qualifying phrase is reminiscent of the missing slot in a PLANES concept case frame. PLANES, however, can only fit missing slots in the sentence, whereas in this example the slot is missing from a noun-phrase. Notice that this is not ellipsis because the preposition "in" occurs nowhere in the discourse. Klappholz and Lockman describe the connection between "the Conservative candidate" and "the election" as a 'reference relation'. A reference via such a relation requires that the context contain, not just some previous words or meaning to be substituted into the sentence, but a previous reference or preset value.

6.3 Pronominal reference

6.3.1 ISA and IRA distinguished

A pronoun, in contrast to a substitute, can refer back to a value rather than a meaning. We call such pronouns "Identity of Reference Anaphora" (IRA) as opposed to "Identity of Sense Anaphora" (ISA).

We can illustrate the distinction more clearly with an example from Hirst [23], page 28:

> "Ross made a gherkin sandwich and ate *it*."
> (IRA: "it" refers to the very same sandwich that Ross made.)

> "The man who gave his paycheck to his wife was wiser than the man who gave *it* to his mistress."
> (ISA: Clearly "it" means the second man's paycheck, not the first man's.)

The distinction between ISA and IRA becomes particularly important when the database, like SHRDLU's, is changing. Consider the following interaction:

"Pick up a block in the box"
(SHRDLU picks it up)
"Put *it* on the table"

(There is now no block in the box, so the description "block in the box" has no reference; however, SHRDLU still knows which block "it" refers to).

SHRDLU deals with IRA in general by recording the variable bindings every time an answer is found. Thus the meaning of the phrase "the block in the box" includes a pointer to its referent for use in IRA pronominal reference. However, the meaning itself can still be used without the pointer for ISA reference;

"Pick up the block in the box."
"Pick up the one in the other box."

No other system implements IRA reference, because the distinction is much less important in a database which cannot be updated during a dialogue.

One interesting feature of SHRDLU is its ability to deal with IRA reference *within a sentence*. This requires the ability to refer to something which hasn't even been found yet. This feature enables SHRDLU to understand a noun-phrase such as "a block which is bigger than anything which supports *it*". This would become infinitely recursive if dealt with by substitution. A noun-phrase is translated by SHRDLU into a 'goal' in the formal language PLANNER. If $g(X)$ is the 'goal' which translates a noun-phrase (e.g. "3 red blocks"), then $g(X)$ can be evaluated against the database to yield a binding, $(X=\{b1,b2,b3\})$, on the variable "X".

SHRDLU avoids the infinite regression by allowing the pronoun, *it*, to refer to the variable "X" rather than the complete goal $g(X)$.

6.3.2 Pro-verbs and pro-adjectives

Of course, anaphors do not always refer back to nouns. Hirst refers to "pro-verbs", and "pro-adjectives" ([23], p. 19). In fact SHRDLU can deal with pro-acts:

"Why did you *pick up a ball*?"
"To build a stack"
"How did you *do it*?"

This extension to the standard noun-phrase anaphor is possible because SHRDLU records "events" as items in the database.

6.3.3 Complexity of determining the referent of a pronoun

The serious problem in dealing with pronouns is to determine what the pronoun (or anaphor) refers back to. There are a number of purely syntactic rules (e.g. a pronoun in a main clause cannot reference an NP in a subsequent subordinate clause); there are rules of semantic agreement (which can be illustrated by the two sentences "The man fanned the *fire* and *it* leapt up", "The *man* fanned the fire and *he* leapt up"); and there are complex rules which allow us to choose the most likely of two alternative referents (as in these two sentences "The *police* dispersed the demonstrators because *they* feared violence", "The police dispersed the *demonstrators* because *they* advocated revolution").

Neither SHRDLU nor LUNAR look beyond syntactic and semantic agreement. SHRDLU assigns a likelihood to a number of alternatives on the basis of the syntax and ultimately selects the most likely. These two are the most sophisticated of the database implementations, though more recently ASK [48] has exhibited the facility to resolve ISA anaphora to a degree of sophistication at least comparable to LUNAR.

Grosz [18] and Sidner [41] used partitioned semantic nets and frames respectively to select the appropriate *context* for each sentence. Wilks's preference semantics [53] can do a much more searching semantic analysis to decide the best reference for a pronoun. Even by adding together all the various techniques for dealing with anaphora, however, we could not find the referent of every anaphor.

6.4 Conclusion

A quote from Hirst: "Clearly anaphora is a highly desirable component of language. It is hardly surprising then that language should take advantage of all our intellectual abilities to anaphorise whenever it is intellectually possible for a listener to resolve the anaphor. Hence any complete NLU system will need just about the full set of human intellectual abilities to succeed".

An NLU, therefore, must use all possible information available from the syntax, semantics and the applicability restrictions and admit failure in the limit. SHRDLU is at an advantage working in a finite domain; in an infinite domain we must search the current context first and the database second. Clearly applicability restrictions can give better semantic guidance for anaphor resolution than semantic markers or even PLANES concept case frames.

7. THE DATA MODEL

The data model imposes structural restrictions on the NLU. It is, therefore, a very integral part of a natural language enquiry system. A good data model will enable the data structure — the definition of the contents of the database — to be relatively independent of the actual storage structure of the database, which may be altered from time to time for reasons of efficiency.

The relational data model is becoming something of a standard for developing natural language query systems (e.g. PLANES, IBM's TQA [36], EUFID [44] and the databases used for research at Cambridge University [43], CalTech. [48], Bell Labs [15], SRI [19] for example). At Marseille, Lisbon, Ljubljana and Edinburgh, as well as in the current system, the language PROLOG has been used, which is also based on relations.

More sophisticated knowledge representations such as Bobrow and Winograd's KRL are being used for research but are too sophisticated to graft onto current database systems. Certain projects use a more limited model than the relational model: LUNAR used *tables* which restricted the possible range of queries; ASK uses *binary* relations.

The essential component of any data model is the 'data values'. In most data models, data values are clustered into rows in a table. For example,

Relational

Relation	Attribute1	Attribute2	...
Tuple1	Value 11	Value 12	...
Tuple2	Value 21	Value 22	...
...	...	...	...

Entity/attribute

Entity Type	Attribute1	Attribute2	...
Entity1	Value 11	Value 12	...
Entity2	Value 21	Value 22	...
...	...	...	...

Codasyl

Record	Item 1	Item 2	
Record Occurrence1	Value 11	Value 12	...
Record Occurrence2	Value 21	Value 22	...
...	...	...	...

An important extension to these concepts is the data *object* represented by a value. For example, if "1904" occurs as a code for an employer and elsewhere as a date for an order, then it represents a different data object in each case.

To reflect this distinction the relational data model uses the concept of a 'domain' associated with each attribute of each relation. For the above example, we must ensure that the 'code' attribute of the 'employee' relation has a different domain from the 'date' attribute of the 'order' relation. Only if two occurrences of a value are in the same domain do they represent the same data object. (Only if two values are in the same domain, furthermore, are they comparable by '=', '>', etc.)

There are a number of other data modelling concepts, such as primary keys and sets, which have more to do with computer storage than with meaning and are not of particular relevance to an NLU.

However, the attempt to build an NLU where words can only map onto the relational objects, Relations, Attributes, Domains and Values, is too limiting. We have already mentioned the problem of verbs (above, section 2.4). Another example is "manager" which could map onto those tuples of the employees relation, where 'job-title' attribute has value "MGR".

The concept of a 'sub-entity' can be introduced to deal with examples such as "manager". If an entity is associated with a particular relation, a sub-entity of this entity comprises those tuples of the relation which satisfy certain selection criteria.

A concept used by INTELLECT is that of a collection of attributes (e.g. 'street', 'town', 'county', 'postcode') which can be referenced by a single word ("address").

Standing back from particular examples it may be possible that one natural language word, or expression, could map onto any formal query of arbitrary complexity. In discussing a suitable data model to underlie an NLU, we must therefore consider not only the data structures but the scope of any query language that could be evaluated against the data structures. Detailed discussions of query languages occur in the next section, and in Chapter 3.

8. QUERY LANGUAGE

The power of a query language reflects the sophistication of the data model and the intelligence built into the query evaluation routines.

8.1 Declarative language

Assuming the power is fixed, the best query language is the one onto which English maps most easily. It is easier to translate "What customers does Collins serve?" into

(1)   List CUSTOMER.CUSTNAME where CUSTOMER.SMANNUMBER =
                                         SALESMAN.ID
                           and   SALESMAN.NAME
                                         STARTSWITH 'Collins'

than into

(2)   SALESMAN.NAME STARTSWITH 'Collins'
        find SALESMAN via SMANNUMBER using NAME
        (obtain next record of SALECUST set) repeat.

(1) is an example of a *declarative* language†, which simply specifies what item is wanted. (2) is *procedural,* and specifies precisely how to get the required item.

8.2 PLANNER

PLANNER, the language used in SHRDLU, was one of the first declarative languages. PLANNER enables the user to specify what he wanted, rather than how to get it, e.g.

            (AND   (GOAL   (#BLOCK ?X))
                    (GOAL   (#COLOUR ?X RED)))

---

† Not all relational query languages are equally English-like. A *tuple*-oriented relational *algebra* is designed for easier implementation on the database. The above example was a *domain*-oriented relational *calculus.*

(where "#PREDICATE" in a predicate recorded in PLANNER's database, and "?VARIABLE" is a variable) is the program which searches for "red blocks". (Some liberty has been taken with PLANNER's syntax.)

Moreover PLANNER could not only express descriptions such as the above, but also quantification:

e.g.   (FIND ALL ?X   (X)
                             (GOAL (#BLOCK ?X))
                             (GOAL (#COLOUR ?X RED)))
"Find all red blocks"

There are severe problems, however, in combining such bits of PLANNER into a representation for a whole query. These problems are dealt with in SHRDLU in a fairly ad hoc style which is effective because SHRDLU's blocks world is so small.

8.3 MRL

The first attempt to deal with the interaction of quantifiers with negation and conjunction in building up a formal query was by Woods [59]. For example, in generating the formal query for

"List the departure times from Boston of every American Airlines flight"

Woods's system swaps round the quantifiers "the" and "every" yielding

(FOR EVERY X2/FLIGHT : (EQUAL (OWNER X2) AMERICAN);
  "For every American Airlines flight,
  (FOR THE X1/(DTIME X2 BOSTON) : T;
    get the departure time from Boston
    (PRINTOUT X1))).
  and print it."

Syntax: A Rule is "(Quantifier/Selector: (Rule1);(Rule2))".

Woods's meaning representation language (MRL) can also deal with *sets* for purposes of averaging, etc.

"What is the average concentration of silicon in each brecchia?"
(FOR EACH X1/(SEQ TYPEC) : T ;
  "For each type C rock
  (FOR THE X2/
  (SEQL (AVERAGE X3/(SETOF X4/(DATALINE X1 OVERALL SIO2) : T))) : T ;
    get the average of the set of silicon concentrations
    (PRINTOUT X2)))
  and print it."

The problems of the interaction of quantifiers, and the necessity to deal with sets are also discussed in Colmerauer [6]. This theory was put into practice by Dahl [9], and Sabatier [38].

8.4 Constraints on the query language

We have looked at a couple of examples of English-like query languages. It is possible to write a translator that yields formal queries whose structure is completely different from the structure of the English sentence. An example from Warren and Pereira [50] is the sentence;

"A man lives"

which has a predicate calculus representation as

exists(X): man(X)&lives(X).

The translator parses the English sentence in the usual way. "A man" is a noun-phrase, "lives" is a verb-phrase. The translator works by operating on variables which may be instantiated at a later stage.

The "production" for the example sentence is:

sentence(Meaning) → noun_phrase(X,VP,Meaning), verb_phrase(X,VP).

(Terms with a capital – "Meaning", "X", "VP" – are variable.)

In our example, "a man lives", the noun-phrase ultimately yields the following result:

noun_phrase(X, lives(X), (exists(X): man(X)&lives(X))).

The trouble with such an analysis is that the meaning of the noun-phrase has become involved with the meaning of the whole sentence. We cannot extract the meaning of the noun-phrase for purposes of ISA anaphora. Thus with such a translator we could not use the context to deal with a follow-up query such as;

"Which American ship is nearest Dublin?"
"Which is nearest Norfolk?"

because we would have no available meaning for the anaphor, "which [American ship]", in the second query. This problem is discussed in [51].

8.5 General Remarks

We conclude that an NLU requires a high level query language, and that the structure of the language should enable it to represent the 'meaning' of such grammatical constructions as – noun-phrases, verb-phrases, etc. As a general guide we should want it to be able to represent any structure that can be anaphorically referred to.

On the other hand the query language must have all the properties of formal languages:

— A computer (database) oriented vocabulary
— No ambiguities
— Semantic functions that are not dependent on a broader context
— Rigorously defined semantics.

Therefore all syntactic links in the natural language query must be given a rigorous semantic interpretation before attempting to generate formal queries. This involves semantic checks which tie:

— adjectives and classifiers to the head noun they modify
— qualifiers and relative clauses to the head noun, or noun phrase, they modify
— direct and indirect objects and adverbial clauses to the verbs they modify.

It also involves resolving anaphora and finding the referents of definite noun-phrases. It is unnecessary, however, to do any more than this, since further processing simply complicates the NLU.

Thus we would require the formal language to embody enough intelligence to

(1) Manipulate the parse tree.
(2) Deal with non-pragmatic aspects of reference, negation and quantification†.
(3) Generate the necessary procedure calls for extracting the information from the database.

9. DBMS INDEPENDENCE

Because the data model imposes structural restrictions on the NLU it is impossible to create a genuinely portable natural language interface. Particularly in systems such as REL and INTELLECT where the NLU extracts semantic information from the database, the very grammatical analysis must be tailored to the concepts of the data model.

DBMS independence can be obtained by using a high-level data model which maps onto a range of data structures. Thus INTELLECT and EUFID use a high-level query language as an interface which can be tailored to different databases.

Another solution to DBMS independence is that of LIFER. When attached to a particular body of information, such as naval data, English queries are translated into high-level formal queries about *ships,* etc. The application-oriented query language can be interpreted onto a range of different databases. Thus the LADDER system is able to use a distributed database with a different DBMS at each node. PLANES uses registers to store the meaning of a query. The query translator simply extracts these meanings and yields a formal database query. This enables the PLANES parser to be free of the structural restrictions of its DBMS. However, the fixed set of registers does restrict the range and complexity of possible queries whatever the power of the query language itself.

10. TOPIC INDEPENDENCE

Both PLANES and the LADDER grammar are "semantic grammars" which must be rewritten for each database. It would appear, however, that given a new set of

---

† There is not, we confess, a clear distinction between semantics and pragmatics. The force of "non-pragmatic" here is that the evaluation of a formal query should not be subject to dispute ("That is not what the query meant . . .").

subnets, the overall design of the PLANES parser could be carried over to any field of information.

The attempt to create parsers for English which are purely syntactic has largely been abandoned. Second generation language systems (Wilks [54]), all utilise the meanings of words during the parsing process.

A second-generation, topic-independent parser can be built by utilising a generalised semantic system such as Wilks's preference semantics [52] or Schank's conceptual dependency [39]. Two NLUs for database enquiry have been built around preference semantics, one at IBM, Bari [27] and one, still under construction, at Cambridge University [43]. The task of tying a preference system to a database vocabulary is very difficult and complicated.

A more economical, though less powerful, solution is to extract the necessary semantics from the database (REL, INTELLECT, EUFID). However, there is never enough semantic information in the database. In the first place databases often use codes (e.g. "m" for male, "f" for female). The English equivalent for such codes must be added, by hand, to the dictionary. More serious problems, such as English verbs (section 3.3 above) require more work in adapting the NLU to the interface. It appears that the more work done in adapting an NLU to a new topic the better the resulting English language coverage.

Perhaps an example would be of interest. NLUs generally treat the question-word "who" as a request for a person (or employee, manager, etc.). However, in different contexts "who" can mean "which company?":

"Who ordered 10,000 widgets?"

or "which country?":

"Who supported Britain at the UN?"

To deal with "who" a genuinely portable NLU therefore requires at least the rudiments of a preference semantics.

An NLU that is effortlessly transferred will be correspondingly restricted in its understanding of English.

11. PRAGMATICS

Pragmatics is the term for the common sense aspects of answering questions. The application of pragmatics can be dissected into two parts:

(1) Intelligent understanding.
(2) Generating pertinent responses.

11.1 Intelligent understanding
An NLU works its way through an English query following a set of grammatical rules and guided by a set of semantic restrictions until at last it yields a formal

query. Sometimes, however, no answer can be found; and sometimes two or more can.

In these cases the NLU has to be a bit cleverer than usual†.

11.1.1 No answers found
When LIFER fails to parse a sentence it resorts to a spelling correction. If this fails it assumes that ellipsis is taking place.

In general, any NLU will have to relax the rules of syntax and semantics that were initially applied. The facility to be satisfied with fewer and fewer preferences is a particularly powerful feature of Wilks's approach‡.

11.1.2 Ambiguity
Many systems can deal effectively with too many meanings, on the other hand. The REL solution is to try out the queries on the database and see which do *not* yield a null response. SHRDLU's resolution of definite noun-phrases (by finding the most recently mentioned N objects which satisfy the description), embodies the same approach in order to satisfy the presuppositions of the definite determiner.

Pragmatics do have a significant part to play in guessing the correct quantifier hierarchy. In Woods's example;

"List the departure times from Boston of every American Airlines flight",

the quantifier "every" was inserted in front of the rest of the query in the formal MRL representation. If the first noun-phrase was singular as in;

"Who is *the man* behind all our research projects?"

then the quantifier "all" should *not* be swapped around.

One other use of pragmatics in resolving ambiguity is employed in the railway booking clerk system of Perrault [35]. A client might ask the clerk

"What time does the Boston train get in?"

or

"What times does the Boston train leave?"

Clearly, "Boston train" is ambiguous as between "train from Boston" and "train to Boston". The system removes the ambiguity from "Boston train" on the basis

---

† Of course systems do incorporate pragmatic principles in the parser itself, but it clarifies the discussion if such common-sense principles are treated separately.

‡ Wilks's semantics does allow meaningless sentences if forced by the syntax. However, the preference system should, after successful parsing, raise a flag to say that there is something wrong. Otherwise the formal query will simply cause a database error.
"Was Dept X born on 15.3.80?"
(Database Error)

of the *intentions* imputed to the client. Thus when the client asked what time the Boston train left, he was probably intending to travel *to* Boston, so he must have meant the train *to* Boston when he said "Boston train".

The use of pragmatics in natural language understanding is guided by Grice's conversational postulates and implications [17]. There is not, of course, anything approaching a set of algorithms for dealing with the pragmatics of conversation and it may well be premature to create NLUs that reproduce a few such pragmatic features before basic rules of meaning have even been formalised.

11.2 Generating pertinent† responses

The use of pragmatics in generating responses from a database is essential. SHRDLU distinguished three levels of detail — "how-many", "vague", "specific" — appropriate to three kinds of question word — "how many . . .", "what" and "which . . ." respectively. Furthermore SHRDLU avoided repeating in the answer anything already present in the question, thus the query:

"Is there a red cube which supports a pyramid?"

was answered

"Yes, a large one"

rather than

"Yes, a large red cube".

The same pragmatic rule can enable a system to distinguish a question about meaning from a question about the data itself. Contrast;

"What is the part required by client X?"

with

"What is a P140?".

The answer to the first may be "a P140", but this could not be the answer to the second. The second question must be a question about "meta-data": meaning, or organisation, of the data.

It is not, in principle, hard to include some meta-data in the database. The problem, for the NLU, is how to distinguish meta-questions from ordinary ones. SHRDLU's simple pragmatic rule is a good start.

A frequent problem in generating answers is how to avoid giving a long list of items which match a certain description. An approach used in SHRDLU, and also currently being developed at Stanford University [25] is to group items in a

---

† Actually one pragmatic system yields "impertinent" answers. This is appropriate when the information in the database is discontinuous (Siklossy, [42]).

response into equivalence classes according to their data values on a particular field. Thus the query;

"Which ships are more than 575 feet long?"

can be answered

"361 ships with shiptype equal to TKR,
55 other ships with shiptype equal to BLK."

Further work on pertinent responses at Pennsylvania University is entitled "Taking the Initiative". It includes the facility to monitor the database;

User: "Is Smith taking 4 courses?"
System: "No. Only 3 so far. Shall I let you know if he registers for a 4th?"

Taking the initiative is well beyond the capabilities of current commercial NLUs.

12. GENERAL QUERIES

The database only has a restricted body of information, and the system cannot cope with questions whose answers cannot be gleaned from the data. The user and the database must understand each other, and many questions will be oriented towards improving this understanding. An example is the query, "What is a P140?", which was used in the previous section.

In a simple database of a few tables the necessary information could, perhaps, be displayed in a single "help" screen. However, in a complex database the *data model* becomes very important. The contents of the database can be elucidated to the user in terms of entities and properties, or some equally high-level concepts.

Tennant [45] discusses the contrast between the linguistic completeness of a natural language query system, and its *conceptual completeness*. The conceptual completeness is the degree to which the concepts expected by a set of users can actually be covered by the system. Tennant, Goodman and Finin proposed a successor to PLANES called "JETS" [12]. JETS would be able to recognise some concepts that are not included in the database, yielding such responses as:

"There is no data on individual pilots in the database."
"The database does not describe all combat aircraft, only fighter and attack aircraft."

Thus the user would be able to understand why the system could not answer particular questions.

One other contribution to conceptual completeness is to invest intelligence in the database search routines. Thus a BROWSER model ([49, pp. 88–107]) was added to the PLANES system to deal with queries about maintenance problems (e.g. "Why is turnround poor at VF–137?"). A more generalised approach to intelligence in databases is in [14]. This remains a topic of database research, however.

13. REFERRING BACK TO THE USER

It is interesting how computer systems become more garrulous as they perform less well. Because NLUs are still a long way short of perfection they need to check back frequently with the user to

- confirm spelling corrections
- report unrecognised words, and ask for the question to be paraphrased if necessary
- to resolve ambiguities
- to check that the NLU has currently correctly understood a query.

In particular when difficulties arise, the system must somehow constrain the user's response so that communication can be reestablished.

In [5] Codd discussed the facility of tightening up on a dialogue, by offering the user a fixed set of alternatives to select from, e.g.

"In the listing . . . do you want suppliers to be identified

(1) by number
(2) by name
(3) some other way?"

The same multiple choice approach is used by PLANES when accepting new definitions.

When the computer becomes heavily loaded, users may become concerned about their inputs even after a brief delay. LIFER seeks to relieve the anxiety by providing a constant stream of feedback. For example the cursor on the screen follows the parsing operation as it works through an input from left to right.

It is important to enable the user to switch off and switch on some of the system's responses, though, so that he can avoid getting more feedback than he wants!

14. QPROC

Having made a general survey of the modules in a natural language understanding system, we can now take a more practical view of some of those modules and their implementation in a system called QPROC.

The next chapter is called "Formalising Natural Language". It defines the highest level of language which can still be specified by formal rules. The translation from natural language to this formal language should involve little more than parsing and semantic checking ('applicability restrictions').

A greater part of the QPROC system depends on this formal language because it has important consequences for the parser, the power of the natural language system (what range of queries can be expressed), context handling, the data model and underlying query languages, DBMS and topic independence.

In Chapter 4 the formal query language, called D&Qs, is fully defined. In the original QPROC implementation the D&Qs were directly interpreted as formal queries to a PROLOG database. A current implementation is being developed where the D&Qs formulae are converted to an underlying query language, ICL's "RDBMS list commands" [24], which can be executed against an IDMS database, or COBOL files, for example. The converter is written in PROLOG and some of this is illustrated in Chapter 4 with a fuller listing of the PROLOG program in Appendix 3.

In Chapter 5 the parser is discussed with close attention to the applicability restrictions imposed by the D&Qs and the application to which the system is attached. Examples are taken from an application on elections and an application called 'COPSE' about customers, orders, products and stocks (see Appendix 4).

Finally the QPROC implementation in PROLOG is examined with some discussion of the limitations of QPROC and further illustrations of PROLOG as a language for writing parsers.

3

Formalising natural language

1. THE DIFFERENCE BETWEEN NATURAL LANGUAGE AND FORMAL LANGUAGES

Natural language is very different from any formal language. In the first case the meaning of natural language words cannot be formally defined, secondly natural language is ambiguous, and thirdly the interpretation of natural language is pragmatic. We shall review these three differences individually.

1.1 Word meanings

'CUSTOMER' records in a database refer specifically to the customers for a certain business, and a fixed set of relevant facts about them. In natural language, however, "customer" might be used in a variety of senses (e.g. referring to a person "He's a nasty customer"). Natural language includes many vague words, such as "many" in this very sentence. ("Many" contrasts with "few", see Chapter 2, section 4.2. Incidentally the natural language facility to self-refer as exampled above is also impossible to formalise since it results in sentences which cannot be interpreted such as "This sentence is false".)

The first step in formalising natural language is to select (one or more) specific interpretations for each word. For a given application only certain words can be formalised; the others must therefore be excluded from the natural language subset understood by the system.

1.2 Ambiguity

Even when the words have been formalised they may still have more than one meaning. Moreover natural language syntax is also ambiguous. This classic example is a sentence with *no* ambiguous words, but at least three possible interpretations:

"I saw a man on a hill with a telescope."

(I, the man or the hill could have the telescope.)

Another type of ambiguity arises in connection with 'quantifier scope'. "Who placed orders in June and July?", for example, has two possible interpretations:

— "Who placed orders in both June and July?" (where the 'scope' of "Who" is 'outside' the scope of "June and July").
— "Who placed orders in June or July or both?" (which could be expressed as "In June and July, who placed orders?", with the 'scope' of "June and July" 'outside' the scope of "Who").

1.3 Pragmatics

The third difference between formal and natural language is the pragmatic aspect of understanding natural language which was discussed in Chapter 2, section 11. To understand and answer a natural language question we often need to use common sense. For these occasions there are no *rules* — that is why it is called common sense. It is very hard to write a natural language system so complex that it does not appear to be following any fixed rules! Thus it is hard to build common sense into such a system.

2. QPROC OBJECTIVES

The job of natural language understanding can be broken into two parts,

— Formalising natural language.
— Executing formal language statements.

Many recognised techniques have been developed for parsing and executing formal language statements and questions: thus the execution part is better understood. The formalisation part should therefore be kept as small as possible by developing a formal language as close as possible to the structure of natural language.

2.1 Deep structure

The formal language must have an unambiguous formal vocabulary and a unique parsing for each statement. One possible candidate for such a language is a parse tree of the original sentence with the formal interpretation of the natural language words as its 'leaves'.

A refined version of this idea — the "deep structure" of a sentence — was introduced by Chomsky [4]. However, it is now argued by many linguists that Chomsky's attempt to separate the syntax of natural language from its semantics has been a failure (King in [55]).

In the context of natural language front ends there are several arguments why parse trees are not a very satisfactory formalisation. Firstly, of course, a sentence may have many parse trees which have nothing to do with its meaning. For example the sentence,

"I saw a man on a hill with a dark brown suit"

must have three parse trees corresponding to the three interpretations of "I saw a man on a hill with a telescope". However, two of these parse trees could not represent possible formalisations of the new sentence, since this only has one meaning.

Secondly it is necessary to map sentences such as

"Pencils cost £5" and "It costs £5 for pencils"

onto similar formal structures. Such a requirement has driven linguists to propose various 'case' grammars which parse a sentence, not into subject, verb and object, but into a verb and its 'cases'.

In the above examples "pencils" and "for pencils" should both be parsed as the same case ('Objective' in Fillmore's case system, [11]). Similarly £5 should also have a consistent case label between the two examples ('Factitive'). Unfortunately no Universal set of cases has been found and so the possible cases in a sentence depend upon the main verb.

The extension of grammar to include cases, moreover, makes the grammar of a sentence depend upon the meaning of its component words. For a database front end these meanings are relations, attributes and domains (etc.). Thus the case analysis requires, for each verb, a mapping from the verb's cases to attributes of the relation which interprets the verb. (To recognise a case, the analyser needs to use the domain associated with the relevant attribute.) This is in fact how QPROC analyses an input sentence, but such an analysis is nearer formal query construction than parsing.

Thirdly parse trees are not powerful enough to represent a formalisation of natural language because they cannot reflect quantifier scope. Consider the sentence

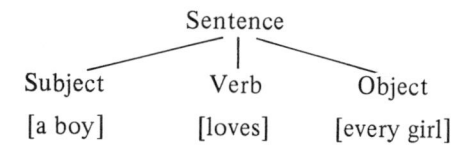

```
              Sentence
         ┌───────┼───────┐
      Subject   Verb    Object
      [a boy]  [loves] [every girl]
```

Strictly this sentence has two possible interpretations, that one boy loves all the girls or that each girl has her own paramour. These two alternatives cannot be reflected in a single parse tree unless it is ambiguous. It cannot therefore be a candidate for the formalisation of a sentence.

2.2 'DESCRIPTION's and 'QUALIFIER's

Instead of using a parse tree as the formalisation of a sentence QPROC therefore uses a logical structure. Sentences are divided into referring phrases ('DESCRIPTION's) and qualifying phrases ('QUALIFIER's). QPROC's verbs map onto database relations, and the subject, object, indirect objects and adverbial phrases map onto attributes. Thus the structure for "Fred lives in London" is:

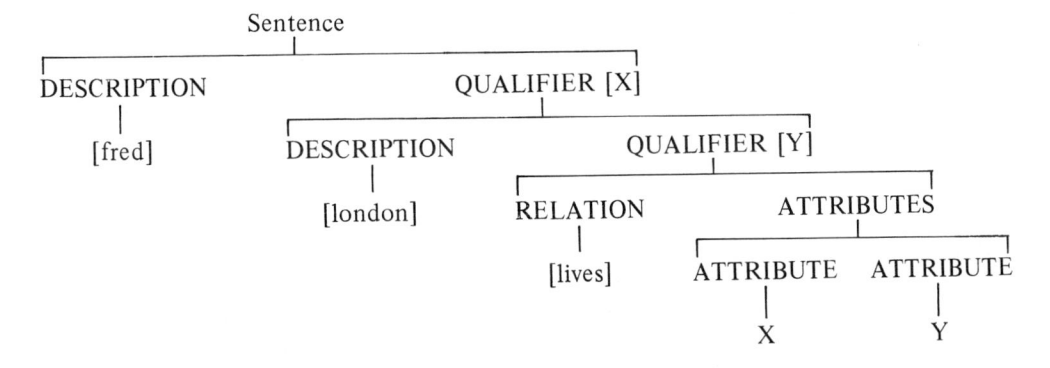

```
                        Sentence
           ┌───────────────┴───────────────┐
      DESCRIPTION                    QUALIFIER [X]
           │               ┌───────────────┴───────────────┐
        [fred]        DESCRIPTION                    QUALIFIER [Y]
                           │               ┌───────────────┴───────────────┐
                       [london]         RELATION                     ATTRIBUTES
                                           │               ┌───────────────┴───────────────┐
                                        [lives]         ATTRIBUTE                     ATTRIBUTE
                                                           │                               │
                                                           X                               Y
```

The order of the DESCRIPTIONs in the structure implies the quantifier scopes.

QPROC's formalisation module is powerful enough to ensure that every parse represents a valid enquiry on the database. It is therefore possible directly to build formal queries without explicitly generating a parse tree. DESCRIPTIONs and QUALIFIERs therefore constitute a formal query language (D&Qs). Clearly the extra work involved in building D&Qs is wasted every time the parser backtracks. This is another reason D&Qs are as high level as possible.

2.3 The facilities of 'D&Q's

D&Qs include a number of features not normally built into query languages. These are the features of natural language which can be formalised and include

- formal determiners
- quantifier hierarchy
- one-at-a-time or all-at-once substitution
- reference evaluation.

These features have also been implemented in various combinations in languages such as Woods's MRL [59] and KS, the formal language in the PLIDIS natural language system ([14], p. 377), and the logical form of [40].

2.3.1

The formal determiners reflect the different meanings of the English words "the", "a", and "which". The word "the" in a noun phrase implies that there is only one unambiguous reference set for the noun phrase. For example "the order placed in June" carries the implication that there is only one June order.

If in a D&Qs query a definite DESCRIPTION (i.e. a DESCRIPTION with formal determiner 'the') has too many referents or not enough, then the formal query yields "presupposition failure". Similarly if a D&Qs query with a "which" type determiner has no answers, it too yields presupposition failure. This failure can be used to reject the current D&Qs interpretation of the natural language query in favour of some other alternative.

2.3.2
The quantifier hierarchy is equivalent to the order of quantifiers in a predicate calculus formula. The query "Who placed orders in June and July?" might be interpreted in two ways in D&Qs:

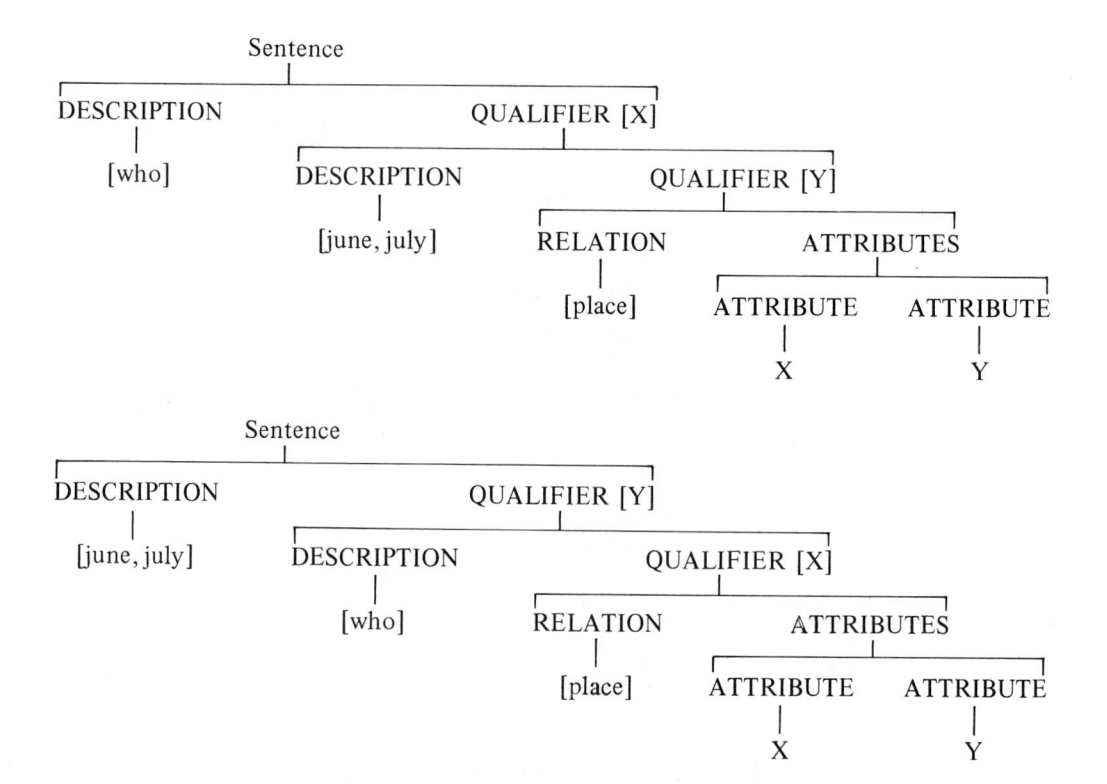

```
                        Sentence
         ┌─────────────────┴─────────────────┐
    DESCRIPTION                         QUALIFIER [X]
         │                ┌─────────────────┴─────────────────┐
       [who]         DESCRIPTION                         QUALIFIER [Y]
                          │                ┌─────────────────┴─────────────────┐
                    [june, july]       RELATION                           ATTRIBUTES
                                           │                ┌─────────────────┴─────────────────┐
                                       [place]          ATTRIBUTE                          ATTRIBUTE
                                                            │                                  │
                                                            X                                  Y
```

```
                        Sentence
         ┌─────────────────┴─────────────────┐
    DESCRIPTION                         QUALIFIER [Y]
         │                ┌─────────────────┴─────────────────┐
    [june, july]     DESCRIPTION                         QUALIFIER [X]
                          │                ┌─────────────────┴─────────────────┐
                        [who]          RELATION                           ATTRIBUTES
                                           │                ┌─────────────────┴─────────────────┐
                                       [place]          ATTRIBUTE                          ATTRIBUTE
                                                            │                                  │
                                                            X                                  Y
```

The first query atempts to find *one* customer who placed orders in both months, whilst the second query takes each month in turn and tries to find the customers who placed orders then. In query languages without a quantifier hierarchy the second alternative must be expressed as a disjunction ("June or July"). However more complicated queries (e.g. "Who placed two or more orders each month last year?") require more drastic reshaping to be expressed without a quantifier hierarchy.

2.3.3
A particular feature of natural language, and of D&Qs, is that mathematical functions like "total" are expressed in precisely the same way as database relations (e.g. "the total of ICL, IBM and AIC's current balances", "the names of ICL, IBM and AIC's salesmen"). To determine the salesmen's names it suffices to look up the names of the salesmen one at a time. However, to determine the "total of ICL, IBM and AIC's current balances" it requires that the balances be taken all at once. Thereby hangs the difference between one-at-a-time substitution and all-at-once.

2.3.4
Reference evaluation in D&Qs is the facility to retain the database items which satisfied each DESCRIPTION in the formal query. This is hard to do for a description which is not at the top of the quantifier hierarchy, since the reference set of a DESCRIPTION low in the hierarchy will be different for each different reference value higher in the hierarchy, (e.g. "In Berkshire and Yorkshire who are the salesmen?"). The result returned from a D&Qs query is thus a tree rather than a table. For a given DESCRIPTION its final reference will be extracted from a number of different branches of the tree (in the above example, the reference of "salesmen" is compounded from two branches, Berkshire salesmen and Yorkshire salesmen).

In the next chapter we define the precise semantics of D&Qs.

4

D&Qs

1. ARRIVING AT D&QS

1.1 Introduction
The concern of this chapter is how natural language sentences map onto the formal language of DESCRIPTIONs & QUALIFIERs (D&Qs). This mapping defines a semantics for the subset of natural language which QPROC can deal with. Because the data model is predefined, and the formal language is tied to the data model, the discussion of semantics will be more restricted than would be necessary for general linguistic purposes.

1.2 Grammar and meaning
The attempt to formalise language was first tackled by logicians who developed the predicate calculus. This formal mathematical language has two fundamental constructions, the "predicate" and the "term". The predicate calculus formula 'ORDER' ('J00026', 'ICL', '19/02/83') has a "predicate", 'ORDER', and three terms, 'J00026', 'ICL' and '19/02/83'.

The natural language noun-phrase has a meaning similar to a term. Natural language clauses also parallel predicate calculus "subformulae" as shown by this example: ('NP' stands for "noun-phrase")

Natural language:

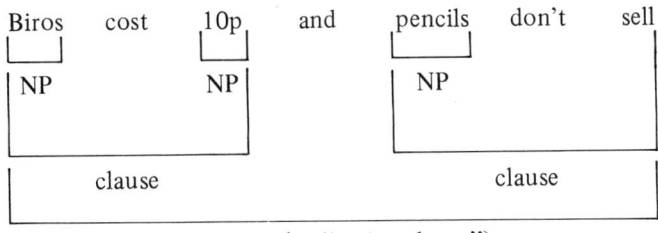

```
  Biros   cost   10p        and    pencils   don't   sell
  |__|          |___|              |_____|
   NP            NP                  NP
  |_____|               |_____|
       clause                            clause
  |_____|
              sentence (or "major clause")
```

Predicate calculus:

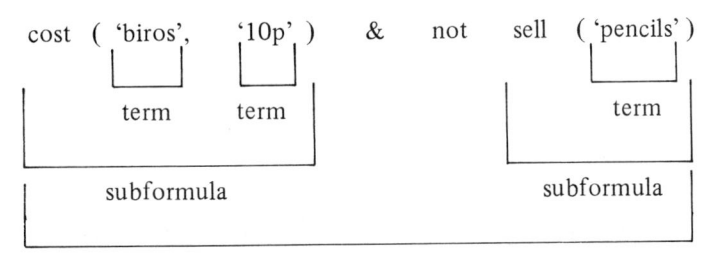

```
  cost ( 'biros',  '10p' )    &    not   sell ( 'pencils' )
         |_____|  |____|                       |_____|
          term     term                          term
  |_____|          |_____|
        subformula                         subformula
  |_____|
                          formula
```

The predicate calculus formula includes two logical connectives:

    '&'   ("and")

    'not'

A more sophisticated predicate calculus concept is that of quantification. Using a variable (e.g. "X") as a term, we can express that "there is an X such that . . .". The symbol $\exists$ means "there exists". It is placed before the variable, and a formula containing the variable, and is written thus:

    $\exists$X. buy(X, 'pencils')

This means that there is somebody (some 'X') who buys pencils. 'X' may occur more than once in the formula. Suppose there is a predicate 'customer' which records where the customers come from, e.g.

    customer('SMITH', 'wiltshire').

The formula expressing the fact that "There exists a customer from Wiltshire who buys pencils" would be:

    $\exists$X. customer(X, 'wiltshire') & buy(X, 'pencils')

At this level of complication the parallel between predicate calculus formulae and the structure of natural language breaks down. We can phrase the previous example more idiomatically thus:

58   D&Qs   [Ch.

Natural language:

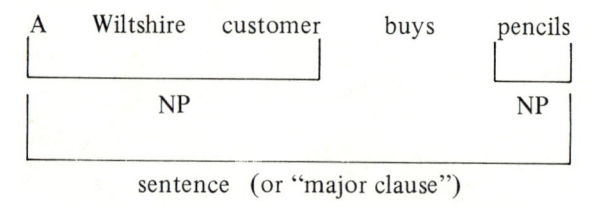

```
     A    Wiltshire   customer       buys    pencils
          |_____|           |_____|
     |_____|      |_____|
                    NP                          NP
     |_____|
                    sentence  (or "major clause")
```

Predicate calculus:

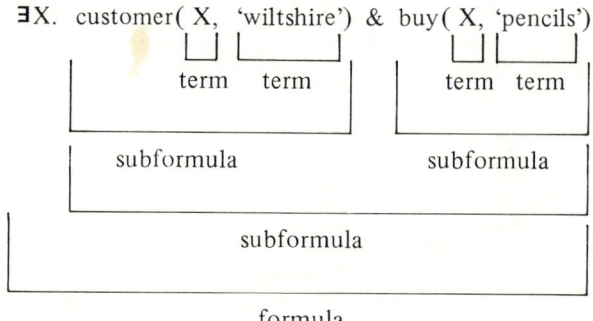

```
     ∃X.  customer( X, 'wiltshire')  &  buy( X, 'pencils')
               |__|  |_____|          |_|  |_____|
               term      term                 term    term
          |_____|       |_____|
                  subformula                    subformula
          |_____|
                              subformula
          |_____|
                              formula
```

1.3 DESCRIPTIONs

To provide a formal language more similar in structure to natural language we introduce the 'DESCRIPTION'. A simple DESCRIPTION is just a predicate calculus term. However, the DESCRIPTION may include a

— determiner (e.g. 'any', whose meaning is very like '∃') — variable
— QUALIFIER containing the variable.

A QUALIFIER is any predicate calculus formula possibly containing a DESCRIPTION wherever the predicate calculus requires a term.
  Now we can express "a Wiltshire customer" as a DESCRIPTION:

    any X. customer(X, 'wiltshire')

This only differs from "∃X. customer(X, 'wiltshire')" because the latter is a formula which is either true or false- whilst a DESCRIPTION refers to a value or a set of values. We can express "A Wiltshire customer buys pencils" as

    buy(any X. customer(X, 'wiltshire'), 'pencils')

The QUALIFIER inside a DESCRIPTION may include DESCRIPTIONs in it. Thus there may be a predicate which defines the counties in the West country: 'westcountry('wiltshire')'. Thus "A West country customer buys pencils" is

    buy(any X. customer(X, any Y.westcountry(Y)), 'pencils')

Just as in natural language we can combine noun phrases with "and" and "or", so too we can combine DESCRIPTIONs. Thus "Good Co. and Better Co. buy pencils" is,

>buy('Good Co' & 'Better Co', 'pencils').

Notice that "Good Co. and Better Co. buy pencils" is not a simple ellipsis,

>"Good Co. [buy pencils] and Better Co. buy pencils",

yielding the conjunctive QUALIFIER,

>buy('Good Co', 'pencils') & buy('Better Co', 'pencils'),

since the verb is not singular. For verbs such as "allied",

>"Britain and France are allied"

yielding

>allied('Britain' & 'France'),

or

>allied('Britain') & allied('France')

it is clear that only a conjunction of DESCRIPTIONs can represent the first sentence since the second interpretation has a different meaning (if any).

1.4 Currying

Before defining "Currying" we shall look at the problems of 'variable scoping' in our current formalism.

For the first example the definite determiner, 'the', must be introduced.

>the X.customer(X, 'wiltshire')

refers to all the customers in Wiltshire. Thus "All the Wiltshire customers buy pencils" is

>buy(the X.customer(X, 'wiltshire'), 'pencils').

Using an embedded description we can refer to all the customers in the West country:

>the X.customer(X, any Y.westcountry(Y)).

'Y' does not refer to a single county, but to each county in the West country in turn. The variable Y cannot therefore retain its value outside the DESCRIPTION in which it occurs.

1.4.1

One scoping problem occurs when a DESCRIPTION occurs twice in a formula:

>"A Wiltshire customer is served by Smith and buys pencils".

We have to treat it like "A Wiltshire customer is served by Smith and a Wiltshire customer buys pencils":

> serve('SMITH', any X.customer(X,'wiltshire'))
> &
> buy(any Y.customer(Y,'wiltshire'), 'pencils')

A different variable, Y, appears in the second DESCRIPTION to emphasise that the variable in a DESCRIPTION has no meaning outside the DESCRIPTION. It is "out of scope". Clearly it is impossible to capture the fact that the same customer who is served by Smith buys pencils.

1.4.2

Another problem crops up when two DESCRIPTIONs occur in a formula. Introducing a new predicate 'salesman' we can write:

> serve(the X.saleman(X), any Y.customer(Y, 'wiltshire'))

"All the salesmen serve a customer in Wiltshire".

However, this sentence is ambiguous. Does it assert that all the salesman serve a particular Wiltshire customer, or merely that they all serve possibly different Wiltshire customers? The problem is again one of scoping. Should one choose the customer first and then check if the salesmen all serve him, or should each salesman be taken in turn to see if he serves any Wiltshire customer? Since D&Qs is a formal language the scoping *must* be unambiguously defined.

1.4.3

So that D&Qs has the power to represent each alternative meaning when required, we introduce a new syntax for QUALIFIERS:

> QUALIFIER ::— not ⟨QUALIFIER⟩.
> QUALIFIER ::— ⟨QUALIFIER⟩ & ⟨QUALIFIER⟩.
> QUALIFIER ::— ⟨QUALIFIER⟩ or ⟨QUALIFIER⟩.
> QUALIFIER ::— ⟨DESCRIPTION⟩ is qual(⟨VARIABLE⟩,⟨QUALIFIER⟩).

This notation is as follows:

> LHS ::— RHS.   The left-hand side is defined by the right-hand side.
> ⟨NON-TERMINAL⟩   Non-terminals on the RHS are put in angled brackets.

The structure 'qual(⟨VARIABLE⟩,⟨QUALIFIER⟩)' is called a "Curried QUALIFIER". The concept of taking a formula and letting one of its terms vary so that it becomes a function of that variable is known as "Currying" after Professor H. B. Curry. Less pungently(!) it is also termed "Lambda abstraction".

Using the new syntax we can represent the problem examples unambiguously as:

"A Wiltshire customer is served by Smith and buys pencils",
any X.customer(X, 'wiltshire') is qual(V, serve('SMITH',V) & buy(V, 'pencils')).
"All the salemen serve a particular customer in Wiltshire",
any X.customer(X, 'wiltshire') is qual(V, the Y. salesman(Y) is qual(W, serve(W, V))).

The first formula above uses the variable 'V' to "represent" the customer in the rest of the formula. In a sense this variable interprets a pronoun and perhaps a closer English rendering of the formula is, "A Wiltshire customer is served by Smith and *he* buys pencils". An example of a sentence with two pronouns is:

"Jack loves Jill and she loves him",
'JACK' is qual(V, 'JILL' is qual(W, love(V,W) & love(W,V))).

(I apologise for the rather sugary example!)

1.5 Relations and attributes

In the previous sections predicates and their arguments have been represented in the form, ⟨PREDICATE⟩ (⟨ARGUMENT⟩, ⟨ARGUMENT⟩, ...). A constraint on D&Qs, however, is that they should interface to a relational database. The relational data model specifies that the attributes are not in any order, but are identified by attribute name. To access a specific tuple in a database it is necessary to select on the relevant attributes. This is generally done by naming the attribute, a comparison operator and a value. The comparison operators are $=, >, <, \geq, \leq, \neq$.

Since D&Qs do not use tuple variables, the same tuple can only be referred to twice in a formula by giving values for all its key attributes. Thus the simplest D&Qs QUALIFIER may comprise a list of selections, e.g.

customer(name = 'Anyco', balance > 1000, county = 'berkshire').

To return a value from a simple QUALIFIER, a variable is used in D&Qs. For example,

customer(custname = X, balance > 1000, county = 'berkshire')

returns the value 'Anyco' if this tuple occurs in the database:

customer	custname	balance	county
	'Anyco'	1500	'berkshire'
	...	...	...

The jargon says that "the formula is satisfied by the association X ≡ 'Anyco'."

1.6 PROLOG evaluation

The programming language PROLOG is particularly apt for getting a computer to evaluate logical formulae. In English, it stands for 'PROgramming in LOGic', but the language was initially developed at France's Marseilles University. Curiously enough, Hungary was one of the earliest countries to recognise its potential for more than pure academic research. Since then its adoption as the programming language for Japan's Fifth Generation Project has established its reputation worldwide.

In the remainder of the book several PROLOG programs will be exhibited, and in section 3 of this chapter the evaluation of a program will be explained by using PROLOG's tracing facilities. A brief introduction to PROLOG is given in Appendix 5.

The evaluation of a simple QUALIFIER can be described in a PROLOG program, if we provide a database of PROLOG facts. Each relation maps onto a PROLOG predicate, and each tuple of the relation is a PROLOG clause for that predicate. This was how the database was stored in the pilot QPROC system. For example the information about products was stored as a series of facts with functor, "product", and four components:

      product(penc1500, 'pencils in packets', 200, 10).
      product(rusq0001, 'square indiarubbers',150, 5).
      . . .

The PROLOG "data dictionary" associated the different components with attribute names. The syntax of the data dictionary was somewhat arcane:

      attribute([product,P,_,_,_], id=P).
      attribute([product,_,D,_,_], productdesc=D).
      attribute([product,_,_,Pr,_], unitprice=Pr).
      attribute([product,_,_,_,U], unitofissue=U).

The data dictionary is used by a PROLOG predicate called "retrieve" which is used to execute simple QUALIFIERs, as defined in section 1.5 above, against a PROLOG database containing only predicates and arguments. The definition of "retrieve" is as follows,

(1)   retrieve(product(Att=Value)) :—
(2)   attribute([product | Arguments], Att=Value),
(3)   Data = . . [product | Arguments],
(4)   call(Data).

Take the four lines of the PROLOG clause one at a time:

(1) This clause head matches any simple QUALIFIER with relation, 'product' and one selection.
(2) The data dictionary is accessed to find out how many arguments the predicate 'product' requires, and which component supports the attribute, 'Att'.

(3) The built-in PROLOG predicate "= . ." is called to convert the list, [product | Arguments] into a PROLOG structure.
(4) The structure produced by (3) is called as a PROLOG goal.

A call of

"retrieve(product(unitprice=200))"

would result in a call of

"product(_,_,200,_)",

which would succeed against the PROLOG database partially listed above.

In its full generality, as required to execute any simple QUALIFIER against the database, the predicate "retrieve" has the following clauses:

retrieve(SimpleQual) :—
    SimpleQual = . . [Relation | List],
    attribute([Relation | FullArgList],_),
    !,
    match(List, [Relation | FullArgList]).
match([Att=Value | Tail], List) :—
    !,
    attribute(List, Att=Value),
    match(Tail,List).
match([NotEqual | Tail], List) :—
    NotEqual = . . [Comp,Att,Value],
    Test = . . [Comp,Value2,Value],
    nonvar(Value),
    attribute(List, Att=Value2),
    match(Tail, List),
    call(Test).
match([ ],List) :—
    Data = . . List,
    call(Data).

It may be instructive for the reader to follow through a call of,

retrieve(product(productdesc=D, unitprice>260, id=penc1500))

(which fails against both of the clauses for "product" listed above).

1.7 Natural language functions

"Natural language functions" are a further sort of DESCRIPTION. The requirement for "natural language functions" comes from examples like: "The customers in Wiltshire and Berkshire". The DESCRIPTION interpreting this phrase must be,

the X. ('wiltshire'&'berkshire' is qual(V,
                  customer(custname=X, county=V)))

This has no reference however because no customer comes from both counties at the same time. Technically this DESCRIPTION is only satisfied if the database contains two tuples:

customer	custname	balance	county
	X	...	'wiltshire'
	...	...	...
	X	...	'berkshire'

where 'X' stands for the same name. Clearly if 'custname' is an identifying attribute then the same X cannot occur in separate tuples. This particular example can be expressed by the D&Qs DESCRIPTION,

the X.customer(custname=X,county='wiltshire') &
the Y.customer(custname=Y, county='berkshire')

however, the problem cannot always be got around. Consider "the customers for any product" in the context "Have all the customers for any product complained?"

The DESCRIPTION,

the X. (any Y.product(id=Y) is qual(V, buy(buycust=X,
buyprod=V)))

refers to all the customers who have bought products. To enable examples like this to be represented there needs to be a way of putting "any Y.product(Y)" outside the scope of "the X". The natural language function enables this. Its syntax is:

DESCRIPTION ::– ⟨DESCRIPTION⟩ is
funct(⟨VARIABLE⟩, ⟨DESCRIPTION⟩).

The two examples can be expressed as follows,

"The customers in Wiltshire and Berkshire"
'wiltshire'&'berkshire' is funct(V,
the X.customer(custname=X, county=V)).
"The customers for any product"
any X.product(id=X) is funct(V, the Y.buy(buycust=Y, buyprod=V)).

1.8 Syntax of D&Qs

To finalise the syntax of DESCRIPTIONs we add 'what' to the list of determiners and we add a "count" so that there is a formal interpretation for phrases such as "Anyco's *three* orders". If the count is unspecified then the interpretation depends upon the determiner. The semantics for the different determiners will be explained below (section 2.3).

We can now give the syntax for D&Qs in the same formalism as was used above:

LHS ::– RHS.   The left-hand side is defined by the right-hand side, (RHS).
⟨NON-TERMINAL⟩ On the RHS, non-terminals are put in angle brackets.
A | B   An 'A' or a 'B' may occur here on the RHS.
A { B | C } D   This is an 'A' on the RHS followed by a 'B' or 'C', then a 'D'.

The full syntax of D&Qs is:

QUALIFIER ::–   ⟨PREDICATE⟩ | ⟨PREDICATE⟩(⟨SELECTIONS⟩).
                        "true" | "person(id = X, age > Y)"
QUALIFIER ::–   ⟨QUALIFIER⟩ { & | or } ⟨QUALIFIER⟩ | not ⟨QUALIFIER⟩.
QUALIFIER ::–   ⟨DESCRIPTION⟩ is qual(⟨VARIABLE⟩,⟨QUALIFIER⟩).
                        " 'berkshire' is qual(V,
                                customer(custname = X, county = V))"
QUALIFIER ::–   true | fail.

DESCRIPTION ::– ⟨CONSTANT⟩.
                        " 'Smith' "
DESCRIPTION ::– ⟨DETERMINER⟩-⟨COUNT⟩-qual(⟨VARIABLE⟩,
                                          ⟨QUALIFIER⟩).
                        "any-2-qual(X, person(id = X, title = prof))"
DESCRIPTION ::– ⟨DESCRIPTION⟩ is funct(⟨VARIABLE⟩,⟨DESCRIPTION⟩).
                        " 'berkshire' is funct(V,
                          the-N-qual(X, customer(custname = X, county = V)))"
DESCRIPTION ::– ⟨DESCRIPTION⟩ { & | or } ⟨DESCRIPTION⟩.
                        " 'berkshire' & 'wiltshire' "

SELECTIONS ::–   ⟨ATTRIBUTE⟩ ⟨COMPARISON⟩ ⟨VARIABLE⟩
                        { , ⟨SELECTIONS⟩ | nil }.
                        "id = X, age > Y"
COMPARISON ::–   = | ≠ | < | > | ≤ | ≥ .
DETERMINER ::–   the | any | what.
COUNT ::–   ⟨INTEGER⟩ | ⟨VARIABLE⟩.

CONSTANT   is a PROLOG atom or integer.
INTEGER   is a PROLOG integer.
PREDICATE is a PROLOG atom.
ATTRIBUTE is a PROLOG atom.

Given certain operator declarations, each D&Qs formula becomes a PROLOG structure.

       'not' must be declared as a prefix operator.
       '&', 'or' must be declared as infix operators.

1.9 Example

This section exhibits the interpretation of the English sentence,

"A professor contested the seat Smith holds in which year?"

as a D&Qs query on the election database. This database was used for the demonstration version of QPROC built at Southampton University as a test-case for my doctoral thesis. The database structure was based on a database used by the BBC for their election-day reporting and analysis. The database is described in Appendix 4.

Throughout the remainder of the book, examples will be taken from this database and the 'COPSE' database, which is used within ICL as an example for illustrating the formal query system, 'QUERYMASTER' [24]. The COPSE database is also detailed in Appendix 4.

The whole sentence is interpreted by a compound QUALIFIER. This QUALIFIER comprises a DESCRIPTION (which interprets "a professor") and a Curried QUALIFIER (which interprets "Y1 contested the seat Smith holds in which year?"). The Curried QUALIFIER itself includes a DESCRIPTION and another Curried QUALIFIER, as shown in the following diagram:

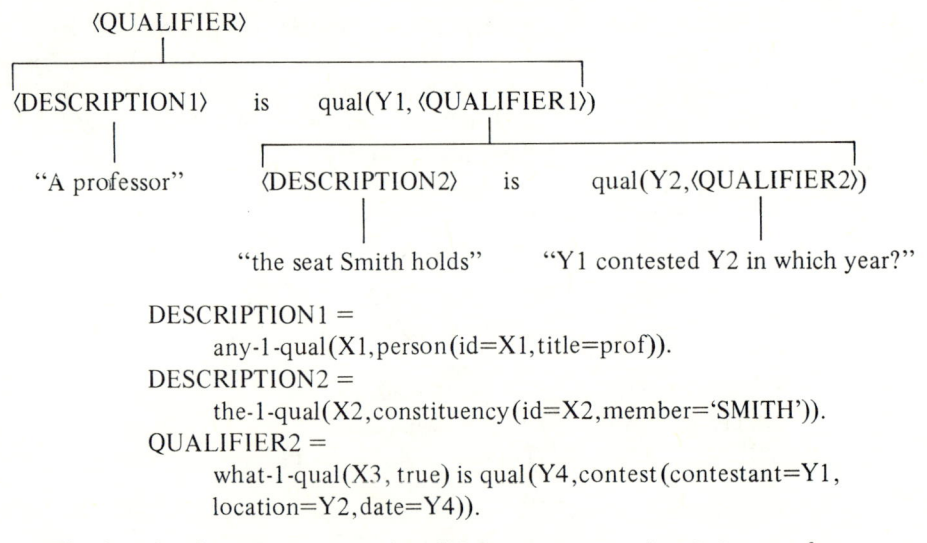

```
           ⟨QUALIFIER⟩
           |
    ┌──────┴──────────────────────┐
⟨DESCRIPTION1⟩    is    qual(Y1,⟨QUALIFIER1⟩)
    |                        |
"A professor"      ┌─────────┴──────────────────────┐
              ⟨DESCRIPTION2⟩    is    qual(Y2,⟨QUALIFIER2⟩)
                    |                        |
         "the seat Smith holds"    "Y1 contested Y2 in which year?"
```

DESCRIPTION1 =
   any-1-qual(X1,person(id=X1,title=prof)).
DESCRIPTION2 =
   the-1-qual(X2,constituency(id=X2,member='SMITH')).
QUALIFIER2 =
   what-1-qual(X3, true) is qual(Y4,contest(contestant=Y1, location=Y2,date=Y4)).

The length of queries expressed as D&Qs is apparent, but it is not of any great concern since the queries are generated by QPROC and are not intended to be typed in directly by users.

2. SEMANTIC CONCEPTS

2.1 Lists, bags sets and atoms

The relations in a D&Qs formula will usually be database relations. However, they may also be built-in predicates not stored as tables, but calculated when required. An example of such a predicate is 'id' which has two attributes, 'subj' and 'obj'. This predicate is used to interpret the English verb "to be" when used to express identity: "Was j0000026 the 29/09/82 order?"

'j0000026' is qual(Z,
    the-1-qual(W, '29/09/82' is qual(X, order(id=W,date=X))) is
        qual(Y, id(subj=Z, obj=Y))).

The predicate 'id' is not recorded as a table but as a PROLOG clause:

id(X,Y) :— X=Y.   /* or simply 'id(X,X)' */

attribute([id,X,_],subj=X).   /* Data dictionary clauses */
attribute([id,_,Y],obj=Y).

When D&Qs formulae are converted into another formal language (e.g. section 3), then these built-in predicates must be recognised by the converter and treated appropriately.

Other built-in predicates implemented in the pilot system are 'equal', 'total', 'count', 'average'. For example 'total' has two attributes 'result' and 'arguments' and is defined by the following PROLOG clauses:

total(0,[ ]).
total(N,[H | T]) :— total(M,T), N is M+H.

attribute([total,R,_],result=R).   /* In the data dictionary */
attribute([total,_,A],arguments=A).

There is an important difference between 'total' and other predicates previously exampled: its second attribute, 'arguments' ranges over lists. (Compare with the 'allied' relation of 1.3 above.)

The meaning of 'total' does not involve the ordering of these lists and in fact 'total' only requires a 'bag' (which is a set with possible repetitions). The second attribute to 'count' and 'average' is also a bag. 'equal' relates two *sets*. However, certain predicates do require an attribute ranging over ordered lists. The best example is the domain predicate which holds of ordered lists of values in the domain. An example might be 'price-down', with one attribute, used in the interpretation of "the products in decreasing order of price"

any-N-qual(P,price-down(values=P)) is
    funct(X, the-M-qual(Prod, product(id=Prod, price=X))).

To reflect this difference each attribute of each predicate has a designated type which is either:

        atom
        set
        bag
or   list

A generic term 'group' will be used for sets, bags and lists. A group will be written as a PROLOG list, [Head | Tail]. If the group is a bag, then [Head | Tail] will stand for all permutations of this list. If it is a set then [Head | Tail] will stand for the set of elements of the PROLOG list.

We also define 'equality' and 'union' of groups:

(a) Equality of groups.

A set is equal to another set, a bag or a list if it contains the same elements as the latter group. Two bags are equal, or a bag equals a list if they contain the same elements each the same number of times. Two lists are equal if they contain the same elements (the same number of times) in the same order.

(b) The union of two groups.

The union of two sets is the set of elements contained in either. The union of two bags comprises the elements of both repeated if they occur in both. The union of two lists is not commutative (L1 union L2 ≠ L2 union L1). It is the result of appending the second list to the first. The union of two groups of different kinds is governed by the definition for the least structured kind. Thus the union of a bag and a list is a *bag*. If L1 is a list, for example, and B1 the bag containing the same elements as L1 the same number of times, then for any bag, B2, L1 union B2 = B1 union B2.

2.2 Satisfying a formula

Let us take two examples:

(1) Relation 'person':

person	id	age	title
	'SMITH'	61	...
	'JONES'	56	...
	...	...	...

The simple QUALIFIER 'person(id=X, age>Y)' is satisfied by the association set X≡['SMITH', 'JONES'], Y≡[50] only if the substituted QUALIFIER, 'person(id=['SMITH', 'JONES'], age=[50])' is true. This holds if the predicates,

person$_{smith}$	id	age	title
	'SMITH'	61	...

person$_{jones}$	id	age	title
	'JONES'	56	...

render the QUALIFIERs 'person$_{smith}$ (age>[50])' and 'person$_{jones}$ (age>[50])' true.

(2) Relation 'total':

total	result	arguments
	21	[9,5,2,5]
	...	...

The relation 'total' would not be held as a table in the database, of course, but calculated as required. The attribute 'arguments' is 'bag valued'. The simple QUALIFIER 'total(result=X, arguments=Y)' is satisfied by $X \equiv [21], Y \equiv [9,5,2,5]$ if the substituted QUALIFIER, 'total(result=[21],arguments=[9,5,2,5])' is true. This is true if the predicate $total_{21}$:

$total_{21}$	result	arguments
	21	[2,4,6,9]
	21	[9,5,2,5]
	...	...

renders the QUALIFIER '$total_{21}$(arguments=[9,5,2,5])' true.

A full definition of satisfaction for D&Qs formulae is in Appendix 2, section 3.

2.3 Formal determiners
The syntax for a D&Qs DESCRIPTION includes,

DESCRIPTION ::− ⟨DETERMINER⟩-⟨COUNT⟩-qual(⟨VARIABLE⟩,
⟨QUALIFIER⟩).

DETERMINER ::− the | any | what.

2.3.1
The simplest determiner is 'any'.

'any-N-qual(V,Qual)',

where N is a count and Qual a QUALIFIER, is satisfied if there is any group with N or more elements returned by the Curried QUALIFIER. If N is variable then the DESCRIPTION can refer to any group with one or more elements.

2.3.2
'what-N-qual(V,Qual)' has the same semantics as 'any-N-qual(V,Qual)'. The definition of satisfaction is, however, indeterminate. A formula might be satisfied in a number of different ways. The difference between 'any' and 'what' is implementation-dependent. There is a possible implementation in which they are treated identically. However, the intention is that the implementation attempts to seek the largest possible reference group for DESCRIPTIONs with determiner 'what', that enables the whole formula to succeed. For DESCRIPTIONs with determiner 'any' on the other hand the implementation may just find the

smallest reference set for efficiency reasons. The definition of the largest reference set for a DESCRIPTION within a formula has not been formalised since it would unacceptably increase the definition of D&Qs semantics.

A further practical use of the determiner 'what' is in mapping the complex D&Qs results onto a simpler format. For full natural language responses a system must take account of the words used in the original natural language query. Less sophisticated responses can be constructed utilising the formal D&Qs representation of the query and in this case the formal determiner 'what' is a useful clue to what would be an appropriate response. In converting D&Qs to simplified 'List Commands' as described below (section 3), the determiner is used by the converter in constructing the 'list of columns' to be output.

2.3.3

'the-N-qual(V,Qual)' is a 'definite' DESCRIPTION. The force of 'the' is that there is a unique reference group for the DESCRIPTION. To define the semantics of 'the' we require the concept of 'presupposition failure'.

When a D&Qs formula cannot be satisfied it fails. This means that the answer to the query is "no", or "none could be found". For example "Who is over 65?" has D&Qs interpretation,

'what-N-qual(X,true) is qual(Y,person(id=Y,age>65))'.

If the relation 'person',

person		age
	'SMITH'	61
	'JONES'	56
	...	...

has no 'age' value greater than 65, then the formula cannot be satisfied.

However, there is another sort of failure which corresponds to the answer

"I must have misunderstood your question".

This sort of failure — presupposition failure — occurs when a DESCRIPTION fails to refer successfully. An example might be "Did the Berkshire customer place an order this month?". "The Berkshire customer" has interpretation

'the-1-qual(X,customer(custname=X,region='berkshire'))'.

If the relation 'customer',

customer	custname	region
	'Good Co'	'berkshire'
	'Better Co'	'avon'
	'Best Co'	'berkshire'
	...	...

has two rows with region 'berkshire' then the reference of "the Berkshire customer" is not unique since it could refer either to ['Good Co'] or to ['Best Co']. (Notice that the reference of "the *two* Berkshire customers" is unique: ['Good Co', 'Best Co'].)

If the reference of a definite DESCRIPTION is not unique, or if the DESCRIPTION fails to refer, a presupposition failure is generated for the relevant DESCRIPTION. This is different from the failure of the whole formula. In practice it results either in an error message to the user, or an attempt to reinterpret the natural language query so as to yield a different D&Qs formula.

2.4 Results
The result of a D&Qs formula has two purposes. Firstly it must record the reference of each DESCRIPTION each way it is satisfied. Secondly the result must provide that correspondence between the answers which is made so clear in a tabular result. For example the query, "What are the addresses of the Berkshire customers?" requires not a list of addresses, but a list of customer-address pairs.

The full result specification is in Appendix 2, section 3.

3. CONVERTING D&Qs TO SIMPLIFIED RDBMS 'LIST COMMANDS'
3.1
In this section we will use three relations for the example query:

customer	id	county

order	id	orderdate

place	custcode	ordercode

The relation 'place' defines which customer ('custcode') placed which order ('ordercode'). The D&Qs interpretation of the English query,

"Which Berkshire customers placed orders on 19.02.83?",

is thus:

'what-N-qual(V1, customer(id=V1,county='berkshire')) is
    qual(Y1,
    any-M-qual(V2,'19.02.83' is
        qual(V3, order(id=V2, orderdate=V3))) is
    qual(Y2,
    place(custcode=Y1, ordercode=Y2)))'.

3.1.1
For a simple English query such as the example, a simpler formal interpretation can be evolved. The simple interpretation consists of a 'rule' and a 'result specification'.

3.1.2
Firstly, if each relation is used only once in the query, then

$$Rel(Att_1=Arg_1, Att_2=Arg_2, \ldots)$$

can be converted to the rule

$$Rel.Att_1=Arg_1 \ \& \ Rel.Att_2=Arg_2 \ \& \ \ldots$$

Each argument is thus associated with a particular attribute of a particular relation. The QUALIFIER,

customer(id=V1, county='berkshire')

yields

customer.id=V1 & customer.county='berkshire'.

PROLOG's unification can be used to actually perform an assignment when the argument is a variable. Thus

customer(id=V1, county='berkshire')

yields only

customer.county='berkshire'

and assigns the value 'customer.id' to the variable, V1.

If a variable, V, occurs a second time in a D&Qs formula, then by the time its second occurrence is ready for conversion it will already be associated with a relation and attribute. The result is that

customer(id=V,county='berkshire') & place(custcode=V)

would yield

customer.county='berkshire' & place.custcode=customer.id

3.1.3
Any constants can be substituted into their Curried QUALIFIERs. Thus if 'qual(V,Qual)' is a Curried QUALIFIER in which the conversion of Qual yields the rule, Rule, and assigns the value 'Rel.Att' to the variable V, then

'Const is qual(V,Qual)'

yields

'Rule & Rel.Att=Const'

Thus

> '19.02.83' is qual(V3, order(id=V2,orderdate=V3))

becomes

> order.orderdate='19.02.83'

and the variable V2 has the value 'order.id'.

3.1.4

A significant simplification is possible if there is no need to preserve the quantifier hierarchy. If N is variable and if the conversion assigns the value Rel1.Att1 to V1, and Rel2.Att2 to V2, then

> any-N-qual(V1,Qual1) is qual(V2,Qual2)

becomes

> Rule1 & Rule2 & Rel1.Att1=Rel2.Att2

(where Rule1 is the result of converting Qual1, and Rule2 the result of converting Qual2). Thus

> any-M-qual(V2, '19.02.83' is qual(V3, order(id=V2,orderdate=V3))
> is qual(Y2, place(custcode=Y1, ordercode=Y2))

becomes

> ⟨Rule1⟩ & ⟨Rule2⟩ & order.id=place.ordercode

where Rule 1 is order.orderdate='19.02.83', Rule2 is null, and the value place.custcode is assigned to the variable Y1.

3.1.5

Adding a global result specification enables the determiner 'what' to be dealt with. If V1 in the DESCRIPTION 'what-N-qual(V1,Qual1)' is assigned the value 'Relation.Attribute' by the conversion, then 'Relation.Attribute' is added to the result specification.

> 'what-N-qual (V1,Qual1) is qual (V2,Qual2)'

converts to,

> 'LIST Relation.Attribute WHERE ⟨Rule⟩'

where the 'Rule' is the conversion of

> 'any-N-qual(V1,Qual1) is qual(V2,Qual2)'.

Thus, finally,

'what-N-qual(V1, customer(id=V1, county='berkshire')) is
    qual(Y1,
any-M-qual(V2,'19.02.83' is
        qual(V3,order(id=V2,orderdate= V3))) is
    qual(Y2,
place(custcode=Y1, ordercode=Y2)   ))'.

converts to:

'LIST customer.id WHERE customer.county='berkshire' &
        order.orderdate='19.02.83' &
        place.custcode=customer.id &
        place.ordercode=order.id'

This formula is a simplification of ICL's RDBMS "List Command" [24].

3.2

The conversion of D&Qs to simplified list commands is interesting as it can provide an efficient implementation of a subset of D&Qs. D&Qs formulae that cannot be converted are those with embedded counts (i.e. DESCRIPTIONs with a non-variable count, 'any-3-qual(V,⟨Qual⟩)'), and those which access a relation twice (e.g. "Who earns more than Smith?").

3.2.1

The converter is an ideal application for PROLOG which is very good at manipulating formal languages. As D&Qs formulae are themselves PROLOG structures (see section 1.8 above), the converter is particularly easy to write. A full version (written for clarity rather than efficiency) is in Appendix 3.

The converter relates each D&Qs formula to a result specification and a rule. The result specification is a PROLOG list, each of whose members is a term of the form 'Relation.Attribute' or 'Const'

(e.g. [customer.id, 'berkshire'])

The rule has the form

    Comp1 & Comp2 & . . .

where each comparison, CompN, is

    Term1 @ Term2.   (@ is a comparison operator, '=', '>', '<' etc.).

Three major predicates that make up the converter are 'convqual' which converts D&Qs QUALIFIERs, 'convrel' which converts simple QUALIFIERs, and 'convdesc' which converts DESCRIPTIONs.

3.2.2
'convqual' has three arguments.

(1) The D&Qs QUALIFIER to be converted.
(2) The result specification produced (a PROLOG list).
(3) The rule produced.

The 'convqual' clause that deals with simple QUALIFIERs is:

/* If ⟨Qual⟩ is a simple QUALIFIER Rel(Att$_1$@$_1$Val$_1$,Att$_2$@$_2$Val$_2$,...)
   then call 'convrel' */
Line A: convqual(Qual,[ ],Rule) :–
                Qual=.. [Rel | Selections],
                relation(Rel),
Line B: convrel(Rel,Selections,Rule).

'convrel' also has three arguments.

(1) The name of the relation.
(2) A list of selections [Att$_1$=Val$_1$,Att$_2$=Val$_2$,...].
    The values Val$_i$ may be PROLOG variables or atoms.
(3) The rule produced.

(Since a simple QUALIFIER can only yield an empty result specification, it is not supplied as an argument.)

The relevant 'convrel' clauses are:

/* For each variable attribute value, assign to the variable the relation and attribute name */
Line C: convrel(Rel, [Att=Rel.Att | Selections], Rule) :–
Line D: convrel(Rel,Selections,Rule).

/* For constant attribute values 'Rel.Att=Value' is added to the ⟨Rule⟩ */
Line E: convrel(Rel, [Att=Value | Selections], Rule) :–
Line F: convrel(Rel,Selections,Rule2),
                conjunct([Rel.Att=Value,Rule2], Rule).

/* To end the recursion, if there are no selections left 'convrel' generates the trivial rule 'true' */
Line G: convrel(Rel,[ ],true).

These clauses deal with the conversion described in section 3.1.2 above. Thus a call of the goal,

    ?-convqual(customer(id=V1,county='berkshire'),ResultSpec,Rule))

yields the following trace (note that we are only tracing 'convqual' and 'convrel'):

```
Line:
A      Enter    convqual(customer( id=V1, county='berkshire'), [ ],
                         Rule)
B&C    Enter    convrel(customer, [ id=V1, county='berkshire'], Rule)
D&E    Enter    convrel(customer, [county='berkshire'], X1)
F&G    Enter    convrel(customer, [ ] X2)
F      Exit     convrel(customer, [ ], true)
E      Exit†    convrel(customer,[county='berkshire'],
                         customer.county='berkshire')
C      Exit     convrel( customer,
                         [ id=customer.id, county='berkshire'],
                         customer.county='berkshire )
A      Exit     convqual( customer(id=customer.id, county=
                         'berkshire'),
                         [ ],
                         customer.county='berkshire' )
```

3.2.3
The next simplification, section 3.1.3 above, comes by substituting constants into their Curried QUALIFIERs. If the D&Qs formula has the form:

'Const is qual (V,Qual)',

the PROLOG converter first converts the QUALIFIER ⟨Qual⟩, then the constant DESCRIPTION ⟨Const⟩ and then it substitutes in the converted DESCRIPTION. Since the DESCRIPTION is just a constant in this case, its conversion is trivial.

The predicate 'convdesc' has four arguments.

(1) A D&Qs DESCRIPTION to be converted.
(2) The 'list command' term ('Const' or 'Rel.Att') which is the reference of the converted DESCRIPTIONs.
(3) The result specification which may be yielded by the conversion of the DESCRIPTION.
(4) The rule produced.

/* Convert a constant DESCRIPTION by returning the constant with the empty result specification and the trivial rule: */

convdesc(Const,Const,[ ],true) :− atomic(Const), !

The 'convqual' clause which converts compound DESCRIPTIONs is:

line 1:   convqual(Desc is qual(V,Qual), Results, Rules) :−
line 2:   convqual(Qual,Result1,Rule1),

---
† Most PROLOG implementations have the unfortunate habit of displaying 'A.B' as [A | B].

line 3:   convdesc(Desc,W,Result2,Rule2),
line 4:   substitute(V,W,Rule3),
            union(Result1, Result2, Results),
            conjunct([Rule1,Rule2,Rule3], Rules).

The meat of this clause is at line 4, when the converted DESCRIPTION, W, is matched with the Curried variable, V. The predicate 'substitute' has two clauses:

/* If the converted DESCRIPTION or the Curried variable is still unbound, unify them, and return the trivial rule */

substitute(V,V,true).

/* But if they will not be unified, then return their equality as a rule */

substitute(V,W,V=W).

Let us follow through the conversion of,

'19.02.83' is qual(V3, order(id=V2,orderdate=V3))

Tracing 'convdesc' and 'substitute' as well, but no longer tracing 'convrel':

line 1: Enter   convqual('19.02.83' is qual(V3,
                                order(id=V2, orderdate=V3)
                        Results,
                        Rules)
line 2: Enter   convqual(order(id=V2, orderdate=V3),
                        Result1,
                        Rule1)
line 2: Exit   convqual(order(id=order.id,
                                orderdate=order.orderdate),
                        [ ],
                        true)
line 3: Enter   convdesc('19.02.83', W, Result2, Rule2)
line 3: Exit   convdesc('19.02.83', '19.02.83', [ ], true)
line 4: Enter   substitute(order.orderdate, '19.02.83', Rule3)
line 4: Exit   substitute(order.orderdate,
                            '19.02.83',
                            order.orderdate='19.02.83')
line 1: Exit   convqual('19.02.83' is qual(order.orderdate,
                            order(id=order.id,
                                orderdate=order.orderdate)),
                        [ ],
                        order.orderdate = '19.02.83')

The first clause for 'substitute', line 4, fails because V already has value 'order.orderdate' and cannot be unified with W which has value '19.02.83'. Thus the second clause for substitute succeeds instead.

78   D&Qs   [Ch.

The last two lines of 'convqual' combine the results and the rules. 'conjunct' drops superfluous occurrences of 'true' from the rule, and 'union' drops duplicated entries from the result specification.

3.2.4

The 'convqual' clause for compound QUALIFIERs also provides for the simplification described in section 3.1.4 above. The only extra clause needed is the one for compound DESCRIPTIONs:

/* The conversion of a compound DESCRIPTION returns its Curried variable. The result and the rule are inherited from the conversion of its QUALIFIER */

line 7:   convdesc(any-M-qual(V, Qual), V, Results, Rule) :−
line 8:   convqual(Qual, Results, Rule).

We can now follow through the example of section 3.1.4.

any-M-qual(V2, '19.02.83' is qual(V3, order(id=V2, orderdate=V3))) is qual(Y2, place(custcode=Y1, ordercode=Y2))

{ The relevant clause for 'convqual' is:

line 1:   convqual(Desc is qual(V,Qual), Results, Rules) :−
line 2:   convqual(Qual, Result1, Rule1),
line 3:   convdesc(Desc, W, Result2, Rule2),
line 4:   substitute(V, W, Rule3),
line 5:   union(Result1, Result2, Results),
line 6:   conjunct([Rule1, Rule2, Rule3], Rule). }

(Tracing 'convqual', 'convdesc', and 'substitute'.)

line 1: Enter   convqual(any-M-qual(V2,
                          '19.02.83' is qual(V3,
                              order(id=V2, orderdate=V3)))
                      is qual(Y2,
                          place(custcode=V1, ordercode=V2)),
                      Results,
                      Rules)
line 2: Enter   convqual(place(custcode=V1, ordercode=Y2),
                      Results,
                      Rule1)
line 2: Exit   convqual(place(custcode=place.custcode,
                              ordercode=place.ordercode),
                      [],
                      true)

line 3: Enter
(& 7)
	convdesc(any-M-qual(V2,
	        '19.02.83' is qual(V3,
	           order(id=V2,orderdate=V3))),
	W,
	Result2,
	Rule2)

line 8: Enter	convqual('19.02.83' is qual(V3, order(id=V2, orderdate=V3)), Result2, Rule2)
Enter	convqual(order(id=V2, orderdate=V3), X1, X2)
Exit	convqual(order(id=order.id,orderdate= order.orderdate), [ ], true)
Enter	convdesc('19.02.83', X3, X4, X5)
Exit	convdesc('19.02.83', '19.02.83', [ ], true)
Enter	substitute(order.orderdate, '19.02.83', X6)

Exit	substitute(order.orderdate,
	   '19.02.83',
	   order.orderdate='19.02.83')

line 8: Exit	convqual('19.02.83' is qual(order.orderdate,
	        order(id= order.id,
	           orderdate=order.orderdate)),
	[ ],
	order.orderdate='19.02.83')

line 3: Exit
(& 7)
	convdesc(any-M-qual(order.id,
	        '19.02.83' is qual(order.orderdate,
	        order(id=order.id,
	           orderdate=order.orderdate))),
	[ ],
	order.orderdate='19.02.83')

line 4: Enter	substitute(place.ordercode, order.id, Rule3)

line 4: Exit	substitute(place.ordercode,
	    order.id,
	    place.ordercode=order.id)

line 1: Exit	convqual(any-M-qual(order.id,
	    '19.02.83' is qual(order.orderdate,
	       order(id=order.id,
	          orderdate=order.orderdate)))
	is qual(place.ordercode,
	    place(custcode=place.customer,
	        ordercode=place.ordercode)),
	[ ],
	order.orderdate='19.02.83'
	    & place.ordercode=order.id)

Thus the final unifications are:

    V2   ≡ order.id
    V3   ≡ order.orderdate
    Y2   ≡ place.ordercode
    Y1   ≡ place.custcode
    Results ≡ [ ]
    Rules   ≡ order.orderdate = '19.02.83' & place.ordercode = order.id

3.2.5

The final aspect of conversion involves dealing with the formal determiner 'what'. The single extra PROLOG clause required to make this conversion is:

    line 9:   convdesc(what-N-qual(V,Qual), W, Results, Rules) :—
    line 10:   convdesc(any-N-qual(V,Qual),W,Result1,Rules),
    line 11:   union([V],Result1,Results).

We convert, "Which Berkshire customers":

    what-N-qual(V2, customer(id=V1, county='berkshire')).

This time we only trace 'convdesc':

    line 9: Enter   convdesc(what-N-qual(V2,
                                   customer(id=V1,county='berkshire')),
                                   W,
                                   Result2,
                                   Rule2)
    line 10: Enter   convdesc(any-N-qual(V1,
                                   customer(id=V1,county='berkshire')),
                                 W,
                                 Result3,
                                 Rule2)
    line 10: Exit   convdesc(any-N-qual(customer.id,
                                 customer(id = customer.id,
                                       county = 'berkshire')),
                               customer.id,
                               [ ],
                               customer.county = 'berkshire')
    line 9: Exit   convdesc(what-N-qual(customer.id,
                                 customer(id = customer.id,
                                     county = 'berkshire')),
                               customer.id,
                               [customer.id] ,
                               customer.county = 'berkshire')

The PROLOG clauses introduced in sections 3.2.1, 3.2.2, 3.2.3 and 3.2.4 have enabled us to interpret the goal,

```
?-convqual(
    what-N-qual(VI, customer( id=V1,county='berkshire')) is
        qual(Y1,
    any-M-qual(V2, '19.02.83' is
                qual(V3,order( id=V2,orderdate=V3))) is
        qual (Y2,
    place(custcode=Y1, ordercode=Y2)
        )
    ),
    Results,
    Rules).
```

which converts the D&Qs interpretation of,

"Which Berkshire customers placed orders on 19.02.83?"

The final unification yields

Results ≡ [customer.id]
Rules ≡ order.orderdate = '1902.83' & place.ordercode = order.id
         & customer.county = 'berkshire' & place.custcode =
         customer.id

3.2.6

The conversion is completed by the clause:

```
conv(DandQs) :-
    convqual(DandQs,Results,Rules),
    write('LIST '),
    writeout(Results),
    write(' WHERE '),
    writeout(Rules).
```

This finally yields:

LIST customer.id WHERE order.orderdate='19.02.83' &
    place.ordercode=order.id & customer.county='berkshire' &
    place.custcode=customer.id

5

Semantics

1. INTRODUCTION

1.1 Purpose

The book contains no specific chapter on grammar. The purpose of a natural language database front end is to enable natural language queries to be evaluated against the data. There is little point in discussing how to uncover the structure of a natural language sentence, therefore, unless the structure can be shown to serve our purposes.

In the previous chapter we exhibited, and to some extent attempted to justify, a formal representation of meaning (D&Qs) which was

(1) suitable for representing the meaning of natural language sentences
(2) executable by a computer against PROLOG databases.

We now analyse natural language in terms of the structures which can be mapped onto D&Qs.

The specific details of parsing such as passivation, and object preposing are not described here. A full description of how QPROC parses a sentence ending in a preposition, for example, would become acutely language dependent, implementation dependent and exhaustive. A clear exposition of a good range of general grammatical phenomena is in [57]. A detailed description of a PROLOG parser is in McCord [29].

We make certain assumptions about the structure of language which will be made clear in section 1.2, but our emphasis is upon how this structure is mapped onto structured data via D&Qs formulae.

A central point about natural language front ends is that the parser should be *domain independent* (so that it can parse queries about cricket just as well as queries about urban planning), but it can be data model dependent so that it maps sentences onto queries which conform to a specific data model. In QPROC, therefore, the words in the natural language subset for a given application will comprise only

(1) formal language words that map onto formal language constructs such as conjunction or quantification
(2) database names or values that map onto relation names, domain values, etc.

In order to move the natural language system onto a new application, the grammar does not therefore need rewriting but the applicability restrictions imposed by the new application (Chapter 2, section 1.3) suffice to adapt the parser to the new vocabulary and the new database.

1.2 Grammar

(a) A sentence comprises a main verb and a number of verb modifiers. E.g.

"Smith contested an election at Worthing"

has main verb "contested" and three verb modifiers, "Smith", "an election" and "at Worthing". (See section 2.1.)

(b) The main verb may be preceded by one or more auxiliary verbs. It may be passive or active, e.g.

"sell", "has sold", "has been sold" and *"has* the product *been sold* ...?"

(c) Various forms of sentence can be recognised such as interrogative − "Is Collins the salesman for ICL?", imperative − "List our customers", and declarative − "ICL placed an order in June" (which is treated as a question). Relative clauses (see (d) below) have a similar syntax to sentences but can't, of course, be interrogative or imperative.

The grammar does not allow sentential complements "I want *to stop now*" or nominalisation "Is *ICL's paying £50 for pencils* recorded?"

(d) The verb modifiers may include a subject and one or two objects (all of which are noun phrases). A verb modifier may also be a prepositional phrase, a relative clause or a specific adverb such as "today". E.g.

subject or object:	"*Pencils* cost *5p*"
prepositional phrase:	"Who is served *by Collins*?"
relative clause:	"Tell me *when ICL order desks*"

(e) A noun phrase may be just a noun such as "Smith" or "£10". However, a compound noun phrase may start with an article ("the"), or a possessive ("ICL's"), followed by a count("1000"), adjectives, classifiers and head-noun ("1974 ICL orders", "creditworthy Berkshire customers").

A noun phrase may be followed by any number of prepositional phrases and relative clauses ("customers *in credit who are served by Collins*"). The grammar does not cover ordinals ("the first order"), complicated counts ("more than 3 and less than 10 orders") or comparative or superlative adjectives ("a bigger order than ICL's", "the biggest order this year").

2. THE SENTENCE, OR CLAUSE

2.1 Verbs and verb modifiers

A sentence has a verb and a number of verb modifiers. The verb modifiers are noun phrases or adverbial phrases that modify the verb. The verb modifiers can be distinguished by their grammar. If one appears before the verb, for example, it is the *subject*; after the verb it is an object.

QPROC's dictionary associates with each verb a database relation and with each proper noun a data value. Thus we can illustrate a simple example of mapping a natural language query onto a database (Fig. 5.1).

Sentence	Smith	contested	which election?
Grammar	subject	verb	object
Meanings	'Smith'	contest	X (variable)

Database	contest	person	election
		'Smith'	'elect1'
		'Bolton'	'elect1'
		...	...

Fig. 5.1 — Mapping a simple natural language query onto a database relation.

In PROLOG grammar rule notation this analysis can be expressed as:

```
sentence(Meaning) --> subj(Value),
                      verb(Relation, Attributes),
                      objects(List),
                      { match([Value | List], Attributes, Args),
                        Meaning = .. [Relation | Args] }.
```

This grammar states that a '*sentence*' comprises:

'*subj*' and '*verb*' and '*objects*'

Each of these must also have a grammatical definition. The goals in curly brackets are ordinary PROLOG goals, which derive the meaning.

For the query "Smith contested which election?", the 'Meaning' would be the PROLOG structure:

'contest('Smith', X)'

and when this is executed against the database it yields the answer X ≡ 'elect1'.

In the sentence

"John bought a car in 1974 in Oxford"

the two verb modifiers "in 1974" and "in Oxford" are grammatically indistinguishable. Their order of occurrence within the sentence might equally well be reversed, so even this cannot be used to make the distinction between them.

However, verb modifiers can be distinguished not only grammatically but *semantically*. When a verb modifier is interpreted onto the database, it is associated with a database domain. In our example database "Oxford" is attached to the data value 'Oxford' which belongs to the 'location' domain. "1974" is a 'date'. Thus

"John bought a car in 1974 in Oxford"

can be interpreted onto the database as shown in Fig. 5.2.

Sentence	John	bought	a car	1974	in Oxford
Grammar	subject	verb	object	in-object	in-object
Dictionary values	'John'	buy1	car	1974	'Oxford'
Domains	person		item	date	location

Database	buy1	Subject	Object	Location	Date
		'John'	car	'Oxford'	1974

Fig. 5.2 — "John bought a car in 1974 in Oxford".

Sometimes the grammatical association conflicts with the domain requirements of a relation. Consider the example the passive sentence;

"A car was bought by John".

In the previous example the 'subject' attribute ranged over 'person'. In this sentence, however, the grammatical subject is "a car" which is associated with the wrong database domain. Without complicating the grammar, this might be dealt with by recognising a separate verb "be bought", with its own interpretation, 'buy2':

Sentence	A car	was bought	by John
Grammar	Subject	verb	by-object
Dictionary values	car	buy2	'John'
Domains	item		person

Database	buy2	Subject	By-object	...
		car	'John'	...

Fig. 5.3 — "A car was bought by John".

The relation, 'buy2', would be a derived relation. The derivation would simply involve renaming the attributes of 'buy1'.

Instead QPROC actually uses a more sophisticated grammar to recognise the "logical-subject" and the "logical-object" of a sentence. Thus both active and passive forms of the sentence can be mapped onto the same relation, 'buy3':

buy3	logical-subject	logical-object	...
	'John'	car	...

This new grammar still misses some useful generalisations. Consider the two sentences:

"John bought a car for Mary"
"John bought Mary a car".

If the first sentence is interpreted as:

buy3	logical-subject	logical-object	for-object	...
	'John'	car	'Mary'	...

then the second sentence will require another derived relation, 'buy4', with attributes "1st-logical object", "2nd-logical-object".

The necessity for two relations, 'buy3' and 'buy4', can be averted by introducing two even more sophisticated categories of verb modifier:

direct-object
benefactive.

A verb modifier is the "direct-object" if:

(1) it is the 2nd logical-object, or the unique logical-object of the sentence,
(2) the relation which interprets the verb has a 'direct-object' attribute,
(3) the verb modifier is associated with the correct domain for that attribute.

A verb modifier is the "benefactive" if:

(1) it is the 1st logical-object (of two), or the for-object,
(2) the relation which interprets the verb has a 'benefactive' attribute,
(3) the verb modifier is associated with the correct domain for that attribute.

These sophisticated categories of verb modifier are called "cases". The cases "direct-object" and "benefactive" can be distinguished on purely grammatical grounds (condition (1) for each case). For many cases both the grammar and the domain check are required to make the distinction. The same (carefully selected!) verb, "to buy", gives an example:

John	a present	for Jane
logical-subject	direct-object	benefactive
John	a car	for $5
logical-subject	direct-object	for-object

Fig. 5.4 – Two different cases with the same preposition, "for".

Cases such as 'benefactive' were introduced by linguists to cater for certain general linguistic situations. As defined here, however, the 'benefactive' case is tied to three very specific conditions. Firstly there is a grammatical condition which corresponds, as far as the current grammar goes, with the general linguistic rules for 'benefactive'. But the other two conditions are specific to the current database application. Only if the underlying relation has an attribute corresponding to the verb case which the linguist would term 'benefactive' can there be a correspondence between the linguist's definition and the use of 'benefactive' in a particular application.

If the 'for-object' maps onto a different attribute from the 'benefactive' then the benefactive must be distinguished from the for-object by the domain check. The benefactive might be described as a "deeper" case than the for-object because the benefactive may be realised in a sentence as a for-object. However, the benefactives and the for-object are *both* cases for the verb "to buy". The definition of the strictly *grammatical cases,* (the logical-subject, logical-object, 1st-logical-object, 2nd-logical-object, and ⟨preposition⟩-object for each preposition), is therefore extended to match the definitions of the deeper cases.

A verb modifier is a ⟨grammatical case⟩ if

(1) it is a ⟨grammatical case⟩ in the sentence,
(2) the relation which interprets the verb has a ⟨grammatical case⟩ attribute,
(3) the verb modifier is associated with the correct domain for that attribute.

All sentences with the verb "to buy" can be interpreted onto a single relation if it has the following attributes:

buy	Attribute	Domain
	logical-subject	person
	direct-object	item
	benefactive	person
	from-object	person
	for-object	money
	instrument	money
	date	date
	location	location

(the "instrument" case can be realised grammatically as the with-object, or the logical-subject).

Some examples of sentences with the verb "to buy" are:

Sentence	John	bought	a brooch	for Jane	from Aspreys	for £500
Grammar	logical-subject		logical-object	for-object	from-object	for-object
Cases	logical-subject		direct-object	benefactive	from-object	for-object

Sentence	Jane	was bought	a gob-stopper	by John	with his last 10p
Grammar	1st-logical-object		2nd-logical-object	logical-subject	with-object
Cases	benefactive		direct-object	logical-subject	instrument

Sentence	That intial investment bought	John	his first property
Grammar	logical-subject	1st-logical-object	2nd-logical-object
Cases	instrument	benefactive	direct-object

Fig. 5.5 — Three example sentences with the verb to 'buy'.

88 SEMANTICS [Ch.

2.2 Mapping verbs onto relations

The linguistic knowledge that enables the cases for a verb to be mapped onto the correct attributes of the underlying relation must be encoded in the vocabulary. The vocabulary entry which gives the meaning for the verb includes

(1) the relation
(2) the attribute associated with each case for the verb.

We can now give a possible vocabulary entry for the verb "to buy". Suppose the database has a relation, 'deal' (Fig. 5.6). The appropriate vocabulary entry for

deal	Attribute	Domain
	purchaser	organisation
	part	part
	seller	organisation
	price	price
	date	date
	location	location

Fig. 5.6 — The database relation 'deal'.

the verb "to buy" would be (as shown in Fig. 5.7). Notice that the query,

"Did X buy Y something?"

will always fail unless 'X' and 'Y' are the same.

```
relation(deal), { logical-subject = purchaser,
                  direct-object   = part,
                  benefactive     = purchaser,
                  from-object     = seller,
                  for-object      = price,
                  instrument      = price }.
```

Fig. 5.7 — A vocabulary entry for the verb to "buy".

Clearly the same relation can interpret other verbs such as "to sell", which has the vocabulary entry shown in Fig. 5.8. (A "recipient" is the 1st-logical-object or the to-object.)

```
relation(deal), { logical-subject = seller,
                  direct-object   = part,
                  recipient       = purchaser,
                  for-object      = price }.
```

Fig. 5.8 — A dictionary entry for the verb "to sell".

If every verb had new and different cases then the grammar could become unmanageable. Suppose some case — such as recipient — is only used for one verb. Then it can be reduced to its grammatical constituents — 1st-logical-object, and to-object. If so the verb "to sell" would have two vocabulary entries (Fig. 5.9). (In fact the direct-object could also be reduced here; to 2nd-logical-object

```
relation(deal), { logical-subject    = seller,
                  direct-object      = part,
                  1st-logical object = purchaser,
                  for-object         = price }
relation(deal), { logical-subject    = seller,
                  direct-object      = part,
                  to-object          = purchase
                  for-object         = price }.
```

Fig. 5.9 — "Two dictionary entries for "sell".

in the first entry, and to logical-object in the second.) This is equivalent to treating "sell" as an ambiguous word with two alternative meanings.

A difficulty occurs if the relation 'deal' does not include any attribute corresponding to some case of the verb "to buy". A solution would be simply to drop that case from the vocabulary definition of the verb. Thus if the relation 'deal' had no 'seller' attribute, the from-object could be dropped from the definition of the verb "to buy" (and, of course, the verb "to sell" would have to be dropped from the vocabulary altogether). However, if the from-object was dropped, the sentence

"Did W. H. Smith buy a computer from ICL?"

would yield a parsing failure, and the query would be rejected.

Therefore a case may be specified as *null*. The entry for "to buy" may thus include:

from-object = null.

With this dictionary entry, the system could parse the example sentence, engage in a dialogue with the user, and execute the query if required.

If the relation 'deal' did not include a 'location' or 'date' attribute, and the query included a location or date verb modifier, then a similar dialogue would take place.

One other advantage of this kind of vocabulary entry is that a case can be mapped onto alternative attributes of the underlying relation, depending on its associated domain. Suppose the database included the relation 'sale' (Fig. 5.10).

sale	Attribute	Domain
	salesperson	employee
	division	division
	item	item
	customer	customer
	price	price

Fig. 5.10 – The database relation 'sale'.

Then two possible questions would be:

"Did Smith sell the widgets to Bloggs & Co?"
"Did division X sell the widgets to Bloggs & Co?"

The verbs "to buy" and "to sell" can be adapted so that the relevant case may be mapped onto either attribute, depending on the associated domain. The vocabulary entry for the verb to "buy" becomes as shown in Fig. 5.11. Similarly

relation(sale),   { logical-subject = customer,
　　　　　　　　　　direct-object   = item,
　　　　　　　　　　benefactive   = customer,
　　　　　　　　　　from-object   = salesperson *or* division
　　　　　　　　　　for-object   = price,
　　　　　　　　　　with-object   = price }.

Fig. 5.11 – Interpretation of the verb to "buy" onto the relation "sale".

the logical-subject of the verb to "sell" is interpreted by:

logical-subject = salesperson *or* division.

2.3 Surface, deep and conceptual cases

There are a number of different case systems, each designed for different purposes, and summarised by Bruce [3]. The case systems fall on a continuum from "surface" cases, (which directly reflect the grammar of the sentence), to "conceptual" cases, (which reflect the meaning of the sentence).

Surface cases are defined by word endings, and/or word order. The classical example is { nominative, vocative, accusative, genitive, dative and ablative }.

The deep cases are supposed to deal with variations in the surface cases which do not affect the meaning. For example, "the door" fills the same deep case in "John opened the door" and "the door opened". However, deep cases cannot provide a representation for the emphasis in a sentence. For example a deep case system would identify,

"Is a block supporting a pyramid?"
"Is a pyramid supported by a block?"

although the "focus" of the two questions is different. QPROC retains a representation of the original order of occurrence of the verb modifiers in the sentence via a different mechanism (see section 2.5).

The conceptual cases enable sentences to be interpreted in terms of a small set of prescribed concepts. The actual words in the sentence are subjected to an analysis which can separate a single word into a number of distinct components of meaning.

As an example we take to the verbs of *change* such as "to open", "to break" etc. Such verbs introduced a change of state, so they involve:

(1) a state (OPEN, BROKEN, etc.)
(2) the concept of CHANGE
(3) the physical CAUSE of that change ("*the key* opened the door")
(4) the INSTIGATOR of the event ("*John* broke the window").

Thus the meaning of any verb of change can be represented in terms of *a state*, a CHANGE, a CAUSE and an INSTIGATOR. Analysis into components can likewise reduce the verb "to buy" into a state (OWNED BY), a CHANGE and an INSTIGATOR.

Such an analysis has been used by Shank [39] in the attempt to reduce the whole of natural language to a fixed set of underlying concepts.

The problems of applying componential analysis are:

(1) That the analysis only approximates to the meaning:
    the fewer the concepts, the less exactly can they represent the meaning. In Quine's view [37] no dictionary definition can be exact so the only set of concepts which can exactly represent all meanings is the complete language!
(2) That analysis into basic concepts is inefficient:
    the single word "election" is an invaluable shorthand for all the activities that make up such an event.

No conceptual cases are used in QPROC because the general concepts – such as CHANGE – will not necessarily be represented in an existing database. A database is just as likely to have a relation which interprets the actual words used in the sentence. In this case it would be more complicated, and less efficient, to allow QPROC to perform a componential analysis of the words used in each query, and then to recombine the concepts so as to map them onto relations in the database.

2.4 The internal structure of verb modifiers

It has been left, so far, unclear what grammatical structure can serve as a *case* for a verb. The logical-object, for example, is generally a noun phrase:

"Smith gained *Worthing* from whom?"
"*Which constituency* was lost by the liberals?".

Other cases are often composed of a preposition ("from", "by" etc) followed by a noun phrase ("from whom", "by the liberals").

Certain verbs, however, include a "that-object" case;

    Frank   hopes   that John is sleeping
 logical-subject   that-object

or an "ing-object" case:

    Fred   enjoys   going to the theatre
 logical-subject   ing-object

Such verbs are interpreted in generative grammar as a predication (see for example [33]) (Fig. 5.12).

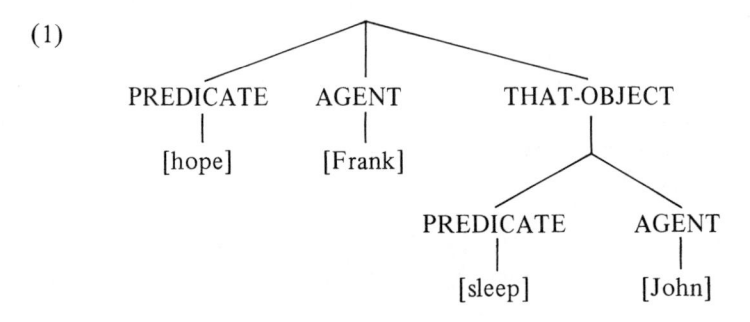

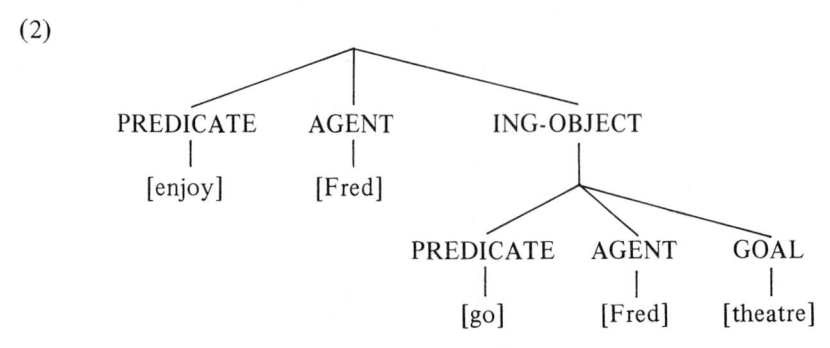

(1)
```
         ┌───────────┼───────────┐
     PREDICATE    AGENT     THAT-OBJECT
         │          │            │
      [hope]     [Frank]      ┌──┴──┐
                          PREDICATE  AGENT
                              │        │
                           [sleep]   [John]
```

(2)
```
         ┌───────────┼───────────┐
     PREDICATE    AGENT      ING-OBJECT
         │          │            │
      [enjoy]    [Fred]    ┌─────┼─────┐
                       PREDICATE AGENT GOAL
                           │       │     │
                         [go]   [Fred] [theatre]
```

Fig. 5.12 – "Predications".

There is no standard way of mapping these onto relations with attributes defined on simple domains. The main predicate in these predications is "hope" and "enjoy" respectively, and their second argument must be a predication. One way of dealing with this is to associate the second argument with the domain of 'events'. Each 'event' value identifies a tuple in an 'event' relation, so clearly 'event's have a fixed set of attributes. Such a technique is not applicable to current relational databases, because there is no such generalised interpretation of an "event".

Research is taking place on the logical representation of events [31] but it may yet be some time before the fruits of such research can be utilised in transportable natural language front ends. Because there is no general semantic apparatus to deal with predications, it was decided that QPROC need not deal with sentential complements ('that-objects', 'ing-objects', etc.). However, any natural language front end must be able to deal with certain words taking constructions of this kind, e.g.

"Is it true that Collins serves ICL?"
"Tell me *if desks are over £50."*

2.5 Interpreting a sentence

The interpretation of a sentence or clause is a formal QUALIFIER in the language of D&Qs (Chapter 4). A simple sentence, or clause, comprises a verb and a number of verb modifiers. The verb is interpreted as a formal relation, and the verb modifiers supply attribute values for that relation. The interpretation of each verb modifier is a pair: '(Grammar,Description)'. 'Grammar' is the grammatical case of the verb modifier, and 'Description' is the interpretation of a noun phrase, (see section 4, below). The simplest form of DESCRIPTION is a data value, such as 'labour', or '1974'. Thus if "to buy" is interpreted as the relation 'deal', the query;

"Did John buy the widget before 1974?"

has an interpretation equivalent to the formal qualifier:

'John' is qual(Y1, 'widget' is qual(Y2, '1974' is qual(Y3,
    deal(purchaser =Y1, part = Y2, date = Y3)))).

Although QPROC's analysis of a sentence does not use surface cases, the syntax of compound QUALIFIERS allows the traditional grammatical categories of *subject* and *verb-phrase* to be mirrored in the formal interpretation. Returning to the example

"Every boy loves a girl",
Desc1 is qual(V1, Desc2 is qual(V2, Qual))
'Desc1' is the formal description interpreting the subject ("Every boy"),
'Desc2' is the formal description interpreting the object ("A girl"), and
'Qual' interprets the verb phrase "[V1] loves [V2]".

Because the formal interpretation reflects traditional grammatical categories, it is very simple to deal with conjunctions such as

"Who was 54 and stood at Worthing?"

"Who" is the grammatical subject and has interpretation 'Desc'. "[Y] was 54", and "[Y] stood at Worthing" are each verb phrases and have interpretations 'Qual1[Y]', and 'Qual2[Y]. Thus the whole sentence is interpreted as

Desc is qual(Y, Qual1[Y] & Qual2[Y]).

Notice that the sentence:

"Who was 54 and who stood at Worthing?"

has a different meaning, and a different interpretation:

Desc is qual(Y1, Qual1[Y1]) & Desc is qual(Y2, Qual2[Y2])

3. DATA MODELLING
3.1 Entities

The query language D&Qs is a domain calculus. This means that each variable ranges over the domain of values associated with an attribute. Each D&Qs constant represents an attribute value.

The interpretation of a noun phrase may be, for example, a simple DESCRIPTION

'Const'

or a compound DESCRIPTION

'Det-N-qual(X,Qual)'

In both examples the reference of the noun phrase is a group of values (a singleton containing the reference of 'Const' in the first case and, in the second, N values which satisfy 'Qual').

The interpretation of a noun phrase is therefore constrained to be a group of values, or a domain variable and a rule. It cannot refer to a whole tuple from a relation. However, it will generally be the case that natural language nouns do refer to some of the relations in a database. In the 'election' database of the appendix, for example, the words 'election', 'constituency', and 'person' all refer to relations. ('Candidate' on the other hand could simply refer to values of the 'candidate' attribute in the relation of that name.)

To enable such relations to be referred to, the QPROC data model is extended to include an *identifying* attribute for these relations. Any reference to the relation is interpreted as a reference to its identifying attribute. A relation with such an identifying attribute is termed an *entity*[†] relation. The domain over which its identifying attribute is defined is termed the entity domain. The introduction of entities to the relational model has been frequently suggested and implemented and it is justified by many reasons besides the above. A good explanation is in [1].

Having introduced entities, we can put them immediately to another use in the interpretation of "implicit joins". An implicit join is required when two relations are used in a query with no mention of how they constrain each other. An example from the election application is

"the candidates in the election of what date?"

[†] Note that no formal definition of 'entity' has been established. The current definition is therefore specific to QPROC.

election	id	constituency	date

candidate	candidate	party	election	vote

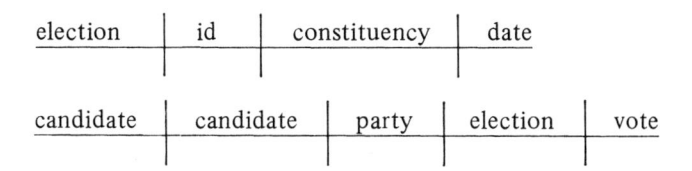

These two relations must be joined somehow to answer the query. QPROC's rule for such implicit joins is that one of the relations, (Relation1), must be an entity, and its identifying attribute ('Id') must range over the same domain as some attribute, Att, of the other relation (Relation2). The constraint which holds between the two relations is that

Relation1.Id = Relation2.Att.

3.2 Domain hierarchies

Another extension to the relational data model is imposed by the necessity to deal with hyponymy (see Chapter 2, section 4.2). Particularly important words in this context are interrogative pronouns such as "who", "where", "when", etc. These words map down onto more specific expressions on specific occasions. Thus in the query to the election database "*Where* did Smith stand?", the specific meaning is "*In which constituency* did Smith stand?"

To deal with such words QPROC admits a hierarchy of domains, at the bottom of which are the actual database domains. The top of the hierarchy includes domains such as 'location' which are independent of any particular database. For each new database the built-in domains, such as 'location', are combined with the database domains (such as 'constituency') into a hierarchy. Two domains "match" if they are on the same branch of the hierarchy. The word "where" maps onto

domain (location).

If 'location' matches 'consistency' then "where" is interpeted as a hyponym of "which constituency". The use of "matching" is described in section 4.3.3 below.

In QPROC the built-in domains are 'thing', 'measure', 'location', 'date', 'person'. Two of these are also domain names in the election database, and so the hierarchy for that database is as shown in Fig. 5.13.

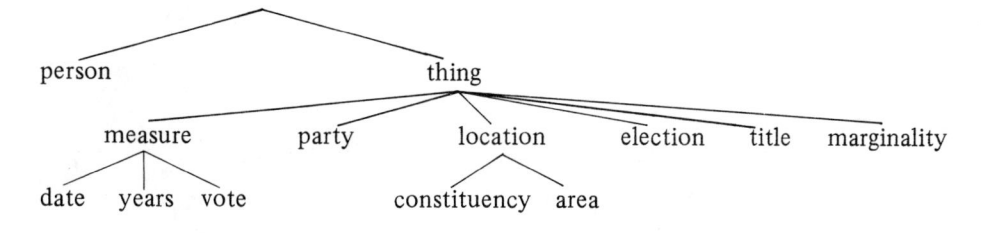

Fig. 5.13 – The domain hierarchy for the election database.

96 SEMANTICS [Ch.

3.3 Base and derived relations

The third extension to the relational model is the distinction between *base* and *derived* relations. The derived relations are those that are introduced purely to support specific natural language words or expressions. Such relations cannot be employed in the interpretation of any query which does not specifically use the word or expression. The base relations are the normalised relations explicitly stored in the database.

We should perhaps mention that third normal form for the base relations is required to underlie QPROC just like formal query languages. If, for example, the election database had all the personal details in the candidate relation shown in Fig. 5.14, then queries like "Count the people with title 'Prof' " would yield

candidate	election	name	title	...
	elect1	'Barron'	'Prof'	...
	elect2	'Barron'	'Prof'	...
	...	...	...	...

Fig. 5.14 – An unnormalized relation.

incorrect replies.

An example of derived relations in the election database is the relation 'contest', introduced to support the English verb "contest".

contest	contestant	election	location	date	party

is derived from, 'candidate'

candidate	candidate	election	vote	party

and from 'election'

election	id	constituency	date

The derivation can be expressed as a single PROLOG clause:

```
contest (C,E,L,D,P):-
    candidate (C,E,_,P),
    election (E,L,D).
```

4. NOUN PHRASES

4.1 The interpretation of a noun phrase

In general a natural language word maps onto any query language construct that could be embedded into the interpretation of the surrounding sentence. A possible approach would be to map each noun onto a domain variable, and a rule. However, the rule can instead be built into a derived relation so that the noun can simply be mapped onto a particular attribute of that derived relation. Thus the possible interpretations of a noun reduce to three:

— a constant (e.g. "Collins")
— a domain variable (e.g. "constituency")
— an attribute of some relation (e.g. "unused credit").

A noun also has a semantic category. For a domain variable, or constant, this is its domain. For an entity name, this is the entity domain. For an attribute name, this is its relation and attribute name. Notice that an attribute also has an associated domain. Syntactically the semantic category 'Domain' is expressed as 'domain(Domain)'. The semantic category for an attribute is expressed as 'Relation.Attribute'.

A noun phrase, like a noun, has a semantic category as well as an interpretation. Generally the semantic category of a noun phrase is a domain.

The interpretation of a noun phrase is a D&Q's DESCRIPTION. For example the following noun phrase

"The date of the election at Newham"

has semantic category 'domain(date)' and interpretation

'Newham' is funct(V1,
  the-1-qual(V2,election(id=V2,constituency=V1))) is funct(V3,
    the-1-qual(V4,election(id=V3,date=V4))).

4.2 Simple Noun Phrases

A domain constant can stand on its own as a noun phrase. Examples from the election database are

"1974" which has semantic category domain(date), and interpretation '1974', and

"Smith" which has semantic category domain(person) and interpretation 'Smith'.

Such one-word noun phrases are termed 'simple noun phrases'.

4.3 Compound noun phrases

4.3.1 Introduction

All noun phrases that do not consist solely of a proper noun are called "compound noun phrases". The analysis of compound noun phrases requires five grammatical categories:

"Article"   (e.g. "the", "both")
"Count"   (e.g. "six", "at least one")
"Headnoun"   (e.g. "election", "age")
"Noun modifier"   (e.g. "southern", "of Smith")
"Relative clause"   (e.g. "whose age is 30", "where Smith was a candidate")

If there are no noun modifiers, the semantic category of a noun phrase is simply that of its headnoun. Thus "10 votes" has semantic category 'domain(vote)'. "Which member" has semantic category 'constituency.member'.

If there are noun modifiers the semantic category of the noun phrase is generally the domain associated with the headnoun. Thus "The member for Newham" has semantic category 'domain(person)'.

The interpretation of a compound noun phrase is primarily a *compound DESCRIPTION*. The syntax of a compound DESCRIPTION is:

DESCRIPTION ::= ⟨DET⟩-⟨NUM⟩-qual(⟨VARIABLE⟩,⟨QUALIFIER⟩).

'DET' is a formal determiner ('the', 'any', 'what')
'NUM' is a variable or an integer
qual(⟨VARIABLE⟩,⟨QUALIFIER⟩) is a D&Q's Curried QUALIFIER.

Clearly, 'DET' is the interpretation of the article, and 'NUM' is the interpretation of the count. For each compound noun phrase a new variable 'VARIABLE', must be generated by the system. The QUALIFIER, 'QUALIFIER', is concocted from the interpretation of the headnoun and relative clauses.

4.3.2 Headnoun
If a compound noun phrase has no noun modifiers or relative clauses, then the QUALIFIER in the D&Q's DESCRIPTION is just 'true'.
Thus the interpretation of "any party" is

    any-1-qual(V,true)

which is the trivial D&Q's DESCRIPTION. The information that V can only range over *parties* is imposed by the D&Q's compound QUALIFIER in which this description is embedded. The compound QUALIFIER is the interpretation of the whole sentence

    (e.g. "Did any party have less than 10 candidates?").

In interpreting the rest of the sentence, the parser utilises the semantic category ('domain(party)') of the headnoun ("party").

If the headnoun were an entity name (e.g. "election") then QPROC could generate a non-trivial QUALIFIER (e.g. election (id = X)), but this would yield a redundancy in the interpretation of the complete sentence.

4.3.3 Noun modification

When a noun modifier is analysed it yields an interpretation, which is a D&Q's DESCRIPTION, and a structure

   (⟨Comparison Sign⟩, ⟨Semantic Category⟩)

which determines how it modifies the headnoun.

  Grammatically noun modifiers can occur in three ways, as:

Adjectives	"The *liberal* candidate"
Classifiers	"The *Worthing* election"
Prepositional phrases	"The constituency *with member Smith*"
	"A date *after 1974*".

Adjectives and classifiers are parsed as simple noun phrases (see section 4.2 above), so their semantic category is that associated with the simple noun phrase.

  Certain forms of adjective cannot be treated as simple noun phrases. These include comparatives and superlatives:

   "A *larger* vote"
   "The *largest* vote".

Also measurements are adjectives, but not simple noun phrases

   "A *27 year old* candidate".

QPROC deals with measurements, but not yet comparative and superlative adjectives.

  Prepositional phrases comprise a preposition and a noun phrase, so their semantic category is inherited from the noun phrase. The preposition gives the comparison sign. Thus the prepositions

   "of", "at", "in", "on", etc. yield '='
   "over", "after", "more than" yield '>'
   "under", "before", "less than" yield '<'

The structures returned by the four examples above (from the election application) are:

"liberal"	('=', domain(party))
"Worthing"	('=', domain(constituency))
"With member Smith"	('=', constituency.member)
"after 1974"	('>', domain(date))

(in the election application, integers between 1800 and 2000 are either numbers, or *dates*).

  The noun modifiers are not dealt with independently. Consider, for example, the noun phrase

   "the vote for labour in the Worthing election".

To interpret this noun phrase, QPROC must recognise that a single relation, 'candidate', links the interpretation of the headnoun, "vote", to the interpretations of the two noun modifiers, "for labour" and "in the Worthing election".

The 'candidate' relation has attributes:

candidate	vote	party	election	...

"For labour" supplies a value for the 'party' attribute, and "in the Worthing election" supplies a value for the 'election' attribute.

The noun modifiers must not be dealt with independently because their interpretations supply attribute values for the *same* tuple of the 'candidate' relation.

If 'X' stands for the labour party and 'Y' ranges over elections at Worthing then the interactions must yield the D&Q's QUALIFIER

(1) candidate (vote = V, party = X, election = Y).

This is not equivalent to the qualifier,

(2) candidate (vote = V, party = X) and candidate (vote = V, election = Y)

since, for example, the labour party might have got vote V in another election, with the liberals getting vote V in the election at Worthing. Such a vote, V, would satisfy qualifier (2) but would not be "the vote for labour in the election at Worthing"!

QPROC ensures that the interdependence of the noun modifiers is dealt with by maintaining a 'core qualifier' throughout the analysis of any noun phrase.

The core qualifier comprises a relation name and a number of selections. When complete it becomes a D&Q's simple qualifier, e.g.

$\quad$ relation(att1 > Var1, att2 = Var2, ...)

The interaction of each noun modifier with the headnoun may extend the core qualifier.

To continue with our example, "The vote for labour in the Worthing election", we consider four stages of the analysis:

(1) "The vote"
    The core qualifier is null at this stage
(2) "The vote for labour"
    The core modifier has relation, 'candidate' and selections 'vote = V', 'party = X'
(3) "The vote for labour in the Worthing election"
    The core qualifier has relation, 'candidate', and selections 'vote = V', 'party = X', 'election = Y'
(4) The whole noun phrase is complete, and the core qualifier is rendered into a D&Q's simple qualifier

$\quad$ 'candidate(vote = V, party = X, election = Y)'

Noun modifiers do not necessarily extend the core qualifier, however. When the noun modifer supplies a value, or direct comparison, with the headnoun, then there is no need. QPROC has a number of built-in relations which are not recorded as tables, but are calculated when required. To deal with noun modification we require the built-in noun comparison relations, 'id', 'gt', 'lt', which hold between two arguments, if respectively they are identical, the first is greater than the second and the first is less than the second.

In the noun phrase "a vote of 1000", the interaction between the headnoun, "vote", and the noun modifier "1000" is interpreted as the qualifier.

$$id(subj=V, obj=N)$$

(where 'V' represents the votes and 'N' stands for 1000).

The core qualifier of "a vote of 1000 for labour" has relation 'candidate' and selections 'vote = V', 'party = X', just as the core qualifier of "a vote for labour".

The interaction between the headnoun and a noun modifier is worked out on the basis of

(1) the semantic category of the headnoun
(2) the core qualifier
(3) the semantic category of the noun modifier
(4) the noun modifier's comparison symbol.

The result of noun modification is

(5) an extended core qualifier
(6) a qualifier interpreting the interaction of the headnoun and the noun modifier.

QPROC generates (5) and (6) on the basis of an analysis of (1), (2), (3) and (4) by cases.

An exhaustive description of these cases would be rather long-winded, so I shall present the analysis in a table (Fig. 5.15). The interaction of modifiers with the headnoun can be compared with the "translation algorithm" of King [28]. A more general analysis is by Finin [13].

4.4 Postmodification and postqualification

Any noun phrase can be followed by qualifying phrases or clauses.

(1) "Smith, *who had been shopping,* was loaded with groceries"
(2) "The election *at Worthing in 1974* was won by the conservatives"
(3) "The emperor *in his new clothes* looked ridiculous".

The first subdivision of qualifying phrases is into attributive qualification (as in example (1)), and restrictive qualification (as in example (2)). Attributive qualification reveals some more about the thing referred to in the previous noun phrase, whilst restrictive qualification has a part in the reference itself. Attributive qualification has no use in query systems and so need not be included in their

102 SEMANTICS [Ch.

Category of headnoun (X1)	Core qualifier	Comparison sign	Category of noun modifier (X2)	Extension to core qualifier	Interaction	Comments	Examples
domain(Dom1)	⟨any⟩	@	domain(Dom2)	null	Comp(subj=X1,obj=X2)	1, 5	A vote *over* 1000
domain(Dom1)	null	@	domain(Dom2)	relation(Rel).Att1=X1,Att2@X2	null	2	Products *less than* £10
domain(Dom)	null	@	Rel.Att	null	Comp(subj=X1,obj=X2)	3, 5	A quantity *greater than* our stock levels
domain(Dom)	⟨any⟩	=	domain(Dom)	null	Comp(subj=X1,obj=X2)	3, 5	Customer balance *below* £50
Rel.Att	null	@	Rel.Att2	relation(Rel).Att=X1,Att2=X2	null	3	Products *with* unit-price £5
domain(Dom)	null	@	domain(Dom)	relation(Rel).Att1=X1,Att2@X2	null	3	Order quantities *after* 1983
Rel.Att1	null	=	Rel.Att2	relation(Rel).Att1=X1,Att2=X2	null		Stocks *with* reorder level over 100
—	rel(Rel),...	@	domain(Dom)	Att@X2	null	3	Stocks in bin 000 *in* which warehouse
—	rel(Rel),...	=	Rel.Att	Att=X2	null		The Berkshire customers *with* salesman Collins
Rel1.Att1	⟨any⟩	@	Rel2.Att2	null	Comp(subj=X1,obj=X2)	2, 4, 5	Delivery date *after* order date

Comments
(1) Dom1 *matches* Dom2 (see section 3.2 above).
(2) Domain Dom1 is associated with attribute, Att1 of relation Rel. 'Dom2' is associated with another attribute, Att2, of the same relation.
(3) The domain 'Dom' is associated with the attribute 'Att' of the relation 'Rel'.
(4) This is an explicit join The domain associated with Att1 matches the domain associated with Att2.
(5) If @ is '=' comp is 'id'.
    If @ is '>' comp is 'gt'.
    If @ is '<' comp is 'lt'.

Fig. 5.15 — Noun postmodification.

semantics. Clearly any qualifying phrase that follows a proper noun (as in example (1)) must be attributive, and so need not be covered. For other noun phrases it is not always apparent whether the qualification is restrictive or attributive (as in example (3)), so all qualifying phrases following compound noun phrases are treated as restrictive.

Restrictive qualifying phrases can be further subdivided into *noun modifiers* and *relative clauses*. A noun modifier is interpreted as a formal DESCRIPTION. The interpretation of a postmodified noun phrase will be given in the next section.

A relative clause, however, is interpreted as a QUALIFIER with a free variable. If the noun phrase has interpretation, 'Det-N-qual(X,Q)', then the QUALIFIER interpreting the relative clause has free variable, 'X'. Postqualification is described in section 4.4.2 below.

The distinction between postqualification and postmodification can be illustrated by a pair of examples;

(1) Postmodification
    "The conservative candidate *in each election*"
(2) Postqualification
    "The constituency *which all 8 parties contested*".

In both examples the initial noun phrase is singular, ("The conservative candidate", "The constituency"); but only in the first example could the whole phrase have a reference set with more than one member. The interpretation of the initial noun phrase has a determiner and a count; 'the', '1' in each case. However, in the second example this determiner and count is preserved in the interpretation of the whole phrase. Only a noun modifier can overrule that initial determiner and count.

4.4.1 Postmodification

The formal interpretation of a noun phrase with noun modifiers is a natural language function. If there are a number of modifiers, with interpretations Desc1, Desc2 ... Descn respectively, then the interpretation is:

    Desc1 is funct(Y1,
        ...
        Descn is funct(Yn,
            Det-N-qual(X,Qual ...)).

where 'Det' interprets the determiner of the noun phrase, 'N' interpets the count and 'Qual' interprets the initial noun phrase and the interactions with each of the noun modifiers (see section 4.3.3 above).

(1) "The liberal vote". The headnoun "vote", is interpeted by a domain name, 'vote'. The one noun modifier, "liberal", has domain 'party'. Its interpretation is, 'liberal'. The relation 'candidate' has the attributes shown in Fig. 5.16. Thus

candidate	Attribute	Domain
	candidate	person
	party	party
	election	election
	vote	vote

Fig. 5.16 – The 'candidate' relation.

the domains 'vote' and 'party' both match attributes of the 'candidate' relation. The core qualifier for the noun phrase is:

candidate(vote=X,party=Y).

The natural language function which interprets "the liberal vote" is thus:

'liberal' is funct(Y,
 the-1-qual(X,candidate(vote=X,party=Y))).

(2) "The 1974 and 1975 elections in Worthing". This has headnoun, "elections", which is an entity, 'election'. The noun is plural so, in the absence of an explicit count, the formal count is left variable, 'the-N-election . . .'. The modifiers are, firstly "1974 and 1975", which has semantic category domain (date), and interpretation;

'1974' & '1975',

and secondly "in Worthing", which has semantic category 'domain(constituency)' and is interpreted as:

'worthing'.

Now 'election' is the entity relation:

election	Attribute	Domain
	id	election
	constituency	constituency
	date	date

Fig. 5.17 – The 'election' relation.

Thus the core qualifier is:

election(id=X,date=Y1,constituency=Y2).

Finally the whole natural language function is:

'1974' & '1975' is qual(Y1,
 'worthing' is qual (Y2,
  the-N-qual(X,election(id=X,date=Y1, constituency= Y2))))

4.4.2 Postqualification

If an initial noun phrase has interpretation 'Det-N-qual(X,Qual1)' and a relative clause has interpretation, 'Qual2[X]', then the interpretation of the whole (noun phrase + qualifier) is:

'Det-N-qual(X, Qual1 & Qual2[X]).

A relative clause is a sentence with a 'trace' in it, thus in the example,

"The seat which Smith holds",

the relative clause is the sentence;

"Smith holds [constituency: X]".

The trace is a hole where something appears only implicitly. Generally a trace occurs when the missing item has already appeared earlier in the sentence. (e.g. Pereira's 'Extraposition Grammars', [34]). The relative pronoun, "which", represents the thing in the hole — 'constituency'. In our example database, this sentence is interpreted as:

'smith' is qual(Y,constituency(id=X,member=Y)).

"The seat" is just, 'the-1-qual(X,true)', so the whole noun phrase "The seat which Smith holds", is interpreted as:

the-1-qual(X,true &
 'smith' is qual(Y,
  constituency(id=X,member=Y))).

A relative clause can also involve postmodification via the relative pronoun, "whose", (or "where" as in many query languages). Consider the phrase:

"The seat whose member is 54".

The relative clause, "whose member is 54", has two parts:

(1) "[person:X1] is 54".
 This is the *postqualification* and has the interpretation:
  '54' is qual(Y1,person(age=Y1,id=X1)).

(2) "Whose member" (or "the member for [constituency:X2]").
 This is the *postmodification* and has the interpretation:
  X2 is funct(Y2,
   the-1-qual(X1, constituency(id=Y2,member=X1))).

The whole noun phrase "The seat whole member is 54" is as shown in Fig. 5.18.

106 SEMANTICS [Ch.

  the-1-qual(X2,

   true

   &

   X2 is funct(Y2,

   the-1-qual(X1, constituency (id=Y2, member=X1))) is qual(Y3,

        '54' is qual(Y1,person(age=Y1,id=Y3)))).

Fig. 5.18 − The interpretation of "The seat whose member is 54".

5. THE VERB "TO BE"

The verb "to be" is three ways ambiguous. The first two interpretations are very similar. They are illustrated in the sentences:

 "Who is Mary?"
 "Who are James and John?"

In English the meaning of "is" and "are" in their respective sentences is identical. The thing, or things, referred to by the subject of the sentence is the same as the reference of the grammatical object. Both "is" and "are" can be treated by case analysis according to the dictionary entries:

(1) rel(id), {logical-subject= subj, logical-object= obj}.
(2) rel(equal),{logical-subject= subj, logical-object= obj}.

The relations 'id' and 'equal' are not part of the database, but they are built into D&Qs (see Chapter 4, section 2.1). These two relations require a different *domain* check from usual because, although any domain matches the subject and object, there is a constraint that the domains associated with the verb modifiers, logical-subject and logical-object, must match each other.

  The other interpretation of the verb "to be" has only one verb modifier, the logical-subject. Examples are:

 "*Worthing* is in the south".
 "How old is *Smith*?"

(The logical-subject is underlined in each case.)

  The predicate is a noun modifier list, and it interacts with the semantic category of the logical subject to yield a formal qualifier. If 'Desc' is the interpretation of the logical subject, and the predicate yields 'Qual', then the interpretation of the sentence is, 'Desc is qual(Y,Qual)'.

  For example, "Which constituency is in the south" has a logical subject "which constituency". This is interpreted as:

  what-1-qual(X,true).

The headnoun is an entity, 'constituency', and the predicate contains the single modifier, 'south'. It yields the qualifier:

'south' is qual(Y2,
   constituency(id=Y1,area=Y2))

The interpretation of the sentence is therefore:

what-1-qual(X,true) is qual(Y1,
   ('south' is qual(Y2,
      constituency(id=Y1,area=Y2)))).

An example of a logical subject which is a simple noun phrase occurs in the sentence:

"How old are Smith and Jones?"

The noun modifier has interpretation, 'what-1-qual(X,true)', and the interpretation of the whole sentence is:
'smith' & 'jones' is qual(Y1,
   what-1-qual(X,true) is qual(Y2,
      person(id=Y1,age=Y2))).

In the query "What is labour?", the single word "what" is a complete noun phrase interpreted as, 'what-1-qual(X, true)'. Its semantic category is domain(thing). ('thing' is a very general domain which, amongst many others, matches the domain 'party'). The query has two meanings. In the first, labour is a simple noun phrase with interpretation, 'labour'.

The 'id' interpretation of the verb "to be" yields the following:
what-1-qual(X,true) is qual(Y1,
   'labour' is qual(Y2,
      id(subj=Y1,obj=Y2))).

For the second meaning, "labour" is interpreted as a noun modifier, 'labour'. However, it yields precisely the same interpretation:

what-1-qual(X,true) is qual(Y1,
   'labour' is qual(Y2,
      id(subj=Y1,obj=Y2))).

Thus no ambiguity results.

6

Implementation

1. INTRODUCTION

In this chapter we shall look at QPROC from two angles. Firstly how QPROC appears to the user, together with some discussion of what is required to move QPROC to another application. And secondly how it is programmed, its architecture and, to illustrate the parser, some more PROLOG code.

2. FUNCTIONALITY

2.1 The Demonstration system

To portray how QPROC appears to the end user, a set of example queries is given in Appendix 1 together with a description of the facilities they demonstrate. The examples are all queries to the election data listed in Appendix 4. This was one of three applications to which the 'pilot' QPROC was applied, the others being a database about archery and an ICL toy database called COPSE ("Customers, Orders, Products and Stock Enquiries"). All three databases were held as PROLOG facts.

The election demonstration was run during 1982 on a PDP 11/34 at Southampton University using Chris Mellish and Lawrence Byrd's Unix PROLOG. The system ran as three separate processes – the parser, the dictionary and the database – communicating with each other via Unix 'pipes'.

The QPROC system is still being developed so we will discuss what it *can't* do in two sections, 'Potential enhancements' and 'Beyond the scope of QPROC'.

2.2 Potential enhancements

2.2.1 Information about database contents

The pilot QPROC system had no facility to answer queries about the contents of the database. It is nearly impossible for an end user to ask questions about information in a database if he cannot ask what it contains! For the demonstration, users were given a diagram of its contents, but clearly such 'meta'-information should be available through the natural language interface.

2.2.2 Context handling

There was *no* context handling. As explained in Chapter 2, section 6 above, complete context handling is an extraordinarily difficult task. Many natural language systems have a facility to deal with pronouns in some limited way, (e.g. LIFER, LUNAR), but no system claims to deal properly with context handling. QPROC's formal D&Q's interpretation provides a basis for a context handling more sophisticated than INTELLECT, LIFER or LUNAR, but the fact remains that the pilot QPROC implementation had none at all!

2.2.3 Terse queries

Natural language queries *are* surprisingly terse. For example, "How old is Smith?" will be longer expressed in any formal query language (e.g. as an RDBMS list command [24] it is 'LIST PERSON, AGE WHERE PERSON.NAME = "SMITH"'). However an even terser form "Age Smith" is still intelligible as a query and can be understood by INTELLECT. Natural language systems can be adapted to deal with terse queries by:

(1) Enabling the system to cope with ellipsis. If a query has no main verb, for example, let it assume that the word "Display" has been missed out.
(2) Introducing a fall-back mode which, if the grammar of the sentence cannot be recognised, attempts to construct a query from the 'content words' in the users input, ignoring the 'function' words (Chapter 2, section 1.1). This is how INTELLECT deals with all inputs.
(3) Adding a degree-of-strictness measure to each construct of the natural language grammar recognised by the system. If an input cannot be parsed, the required degree-of-strictness is gradually reduced so that the strictest rules are waived. Thus the system might initially require singular noun phrases to be preceded by a determiner "List *the* age of Smith", but at a lower degree of strictness this requirement is waived so the system can recognise "List age of Smith". It is important to have the strict rules in the parser to deal with inputs where these rules *do* affect the interpretation of the sentence (such as the distinction between definite and indefinite reference, see Chapter 4, section 2.3). Prof. Campbell pointed out to me that as natural language applications become more wide-ranging such compression becomes increasingly hard to interpret. "How old Fred Smith" may not be a request for his age but his condition: "Fred Smith fine. How you?"

The pilot QPROC system had some facility for detecting ellipsis, but no fall-back mode or degree-of-strictness.

2.2.4 A large built-in vocabulary of words and phrases

QPROC has a built-in vocabulary of about 80 words. When QPROC is attached to an application this vocabulary is augmented by names of relations, attributes, domains and values from the database. It is also topped up with synonyms and other words which may be appropriate for the particular application.

Experiments by Kelly and Chapanis [26] have shown that users of a simulated natural language system can solve their problems as fast with a vocabulary limited to 300 words as they can with an unlimited vocabulary. Chapanis selected three problems (a class scheduling problem, a fault finding problem and an object identification problem) which required the problem solvers to communicate with each other on a teletype. Different teams were allowed to use different vocabularies. An unlimited vocabulary was available to the control group; the larger limited vocabulary included 500 words (425 core words, 75 problem specific words), and the smaller limited vocabulary had just 300 words (225 core and 75 problem specific). The teams with limited vocabularies spent up to an hour learning their vocabularies, and then during the problem solving any message with a disallowed word was rejected. An additional requirement was that the teams who worked with a limited vocabulary had to spell their words accurately. It turned out that vocabulary size had no effect on the time taken to solve any problem, or on the correctness of the solution!

Chapanis notes, however, that "subjects using the restricted vocabularies often exhibited frustration and occasionally anger when a message they had typed was rejected the computer"! In a later experiment, Chapanis found that even when subjects were allowed to communicate verbally, enforced brevity did not affect the time taken or accuracy in solving problems. In fact problem solvers, when financially induced to use as few words as possible, were just as terse in verbal communication as they were under similar conditions on a teletype. However, verbal communication still enabled problems to be solved twice as fast as teletype communication.

In view of these experiments, it appears that a built in basic vocabulary, supplemented by a number of application dependent words, is probably in some sense sufficient. However, to avoid causing the frustration and anger noted by Chapanis, QPROC's built-in vocabulary should be extended in a variety of ways to make the system less 'fussy'.

One currently awkward area is people's names. These can be expressed as:

(1) Mrs Smith
(2) P. J. Smith
(3) Pam Smith

for example.

(1) The basic vocabulary should therefore have "Mr", "Mrs", etc. built-in. These words are followed by a person's name, and should be ignored unless the database includes information about titles or sex.
(2) The parser should recognise initials and throw them away if initials are not held in the database. The occurrence of a full stop after initials is a problem for some parsers (like INTELLECT's) which treat them as punctuation and throw them away — nasty if initials with full stops *are* held in the database.
(3) There are a great number of names which English speakers can recognise from background knowledge. We know "Pam" is a first name which, like titles and initials, may be thrown away if the database only holds surnames. QPROC, however, outputs '???' underneath the word "Pam" to indicate that the word is not recognised. If INTELLECT recognises that 'Smith' is a surname, but does not recognise 'Pam', it deduces from the proximity of the two words that 'Pam' is another surname.

For a natural language system to seem 'sensible' it is important to put first names, place names, etc. into the basic vocabulary so that queries mentioning such names can be understood even if there is nothing with that name in the database.

Clearly there are other particular areas where built-in phrases are necessary: sums of money ("£1.50", "Ten quid"), dates ("10.12.82", "June", "Last week/month/year"), addresses ("10 Pont St, Newtown, Berks", "Dunroamin, Piddletrenthide, Nr Brighton, Yorks").

One final requirements for built-in phrases is to cope with circumlocutions such as

"Please could you tell me if . . ."
"Do you know, by any chance, whether . . . "

Clearly the longer phrases could be avoided by users themselves; but all the same there is a large variety of ways to phrase a question.

2.3 Beyond the scope of QPROC
2.3.1
The first item in this category is the "predication" discussed in Chapter 5, section 2.4 above. This precludes verb modifiers which are themselves whole clauses:

"I love *going to the circus*"

Such modifiers are not necessary for getting data from current databases because current implemented data models do not have 'events' (e.g. 'going to the circus') as possible attribute values for relations.

Predications do arise, however, in the circumlocutions mentioned in the previous section. This is insufficient reason for adding clause-type verb modifiers to QPROC's parser because such verb modifiers bring in many complex parsing issues.

To deal with circumlocutions in such a general way, QPROC would have to transform queries like

"I want to know Smith's salary"

into

"I want ⟨that I know Smith's salary⟩"

Such transformations are really detours on the way to eliciting the intended formal query.

Certain data items stored in current databases can be expressed using predications. For example, "ICL's order for pencils" can be described as an event "ICL's ordering pencils". It seems probable, however, that users do avoid using complex constructions when attempting to express themselves simply and clearly (e.g. [47]).

2.3.2

There is a relationship between actual events (ICL supplies a computer), probabilities (ICL may supply a computer) and possibilities (ICL can supply a computer).

If all three queries are to be dealt with by QPROC, the three constructions 'supply', 'can supply' and 'may supply' must be entered separately, each with its own derived relation. QPROC has no general concept of actual, probable and possible.

There are many other linguistic generalisations, for example the linguistic concept of a verb of change. Such verbs include "open", "learn", "empty", etc. These verbs may have a subject, direct object and with-object — "John burnt the newspaper with his lighter" — or just a subject — "The newspaper burnt". If QPROC categorised all natural language verbs in this way, the cases for each verb could be deduced from its category. However, QPROC does not utilise linguistic generalisations of this kind firstly because they all seem to have exceptions, and secondly because it would require the 'knowledge engineer' to understand them if he were to set up the system on a new application.

Instead QPROC aims to be relatively simple and transparent.

2.3.3

A fully portable natural language understanding system would include a complete dictionary in it. Such a dictionary would give the meaning of each word in terms of other words in the language. When such a natural language system was attached to an application, a particular set of words would be redefined to map onto the application. The dictionary would then be used to map all the other words onto the application.

There is some research going on, on a set of 'semantic primitives' which underlies natural language [39]; however, the fully portable language system is not even on the horizon, it is out of sight. Language is too complicated to allow each word to be defined by other words. None of the definitions are precise enough to enable the definition to be substituted for the defined word in any sentence containing that word. Any attempt to reduce language to a fixed set of primitives will lose part of the meaning of the remaining words (e.g. "tenacious", "stubborn" and "pig-headed" are not quite synonyms!). Finally there are several groups of words which do not have a semantic primitive. One such group is "just", "fair", "even-handed" whose definition has been an object of study for centuries!

3. QPROC DESIGN

3.1 The data dictionary

To set up a QPROC application, an essential component is a "data dictionary". (INTELLECT's data dictionary is termed the 'LEXICON'). This is a file of information about the data. It lists the relations, their attributes, and their domains. It also records some of the data values that may occur in the database, for example the domain 'party' has values:

        conservative
        labour
        liberal
        'SDP'

These values are all recorded in the data dictionary even though, at some instant, one of these values may not occur in the data.

The data dictionary is combined with the system's in-built basic vocabulary to yield the full vocabulary required for this application.

Finally there is a facility to define synonyms for any word.

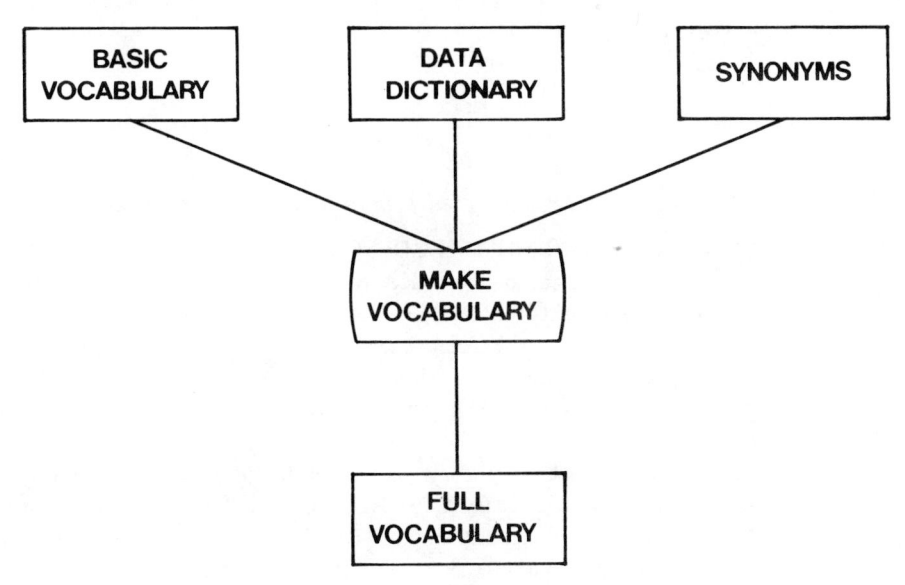

Fig. 6.1 – Generation of the full vocabulary.

3.2 The full vocabulary

In QPROC the full vocabulary and synonyms are stored as a list of PROLOG facts with the form

'&word' (Part_Of_Speech, Continuation, Ending, Meaning)

The functor '&word' is the natural language word preceded by a '&' (to avoid name clashes).

Of particular interest is the 'Continuation'.

An example entry is

'&social' (noun, "democrat", singular&_, party: 'SDP').

The 'continuation' is "democrat" and this tells QPROC to check, whenever it comes across the word "social", that the next word is "democrat".

The task of mapping natural language input onto vocabulary entries is further complicated by inflexions. QPROC must also match "social democrats" and "social democratic [party]" onto the vocabulary entry.

Furthermore, some multiple word entries (e.g. "take offence") inflect on the first word ("takes offence") rather than the last word.

Non-standard endings are dealt with by synonyms. So "took" is entered as the perfect of "take", by giving its meaning as "take":

'&took' (verb, nil, perfect, "take").

The entry will now make "took offence" the perfect of "take offence".

The continuation can be more complicated than just a word, or list of words. It can, for example, be any word with a certain meaning. Thus in the election application the entry for "Mr" enabled any person's name of the form "Mr X" to be parsed as a noun phrase:

'&Mr' (noun_phrase,
    dic(noun, X, _, person: P),
    _,
    desc(the, _, qual(V, person(id=P, title='Mr', id=V))))

(The meaning is a formal D&Qs DESCRIPTION)

Vocabularies can be extended to include more and more constructions, such as idioms "kick the bucket", and 'gapped' words (like "Take over" in "They took the country over"). A complete dictionary entry for the word "and" would practically involve storing a whole natural language grammar to define its meanings in context. (In QPROC the meaning of "and" *is* partly dealt with in the grammar).

At the level of functionality provided by QPROC, it is perfectly effective to store each dictionary entry as a PROLOG fact. The automatic hashing provided by the PROLOG compiler enables the dictionary to have a clear and readable source form, but an efficient compiled form providing direct access to each entry.

3.3 Runtime components
The runtime components of QPROC are

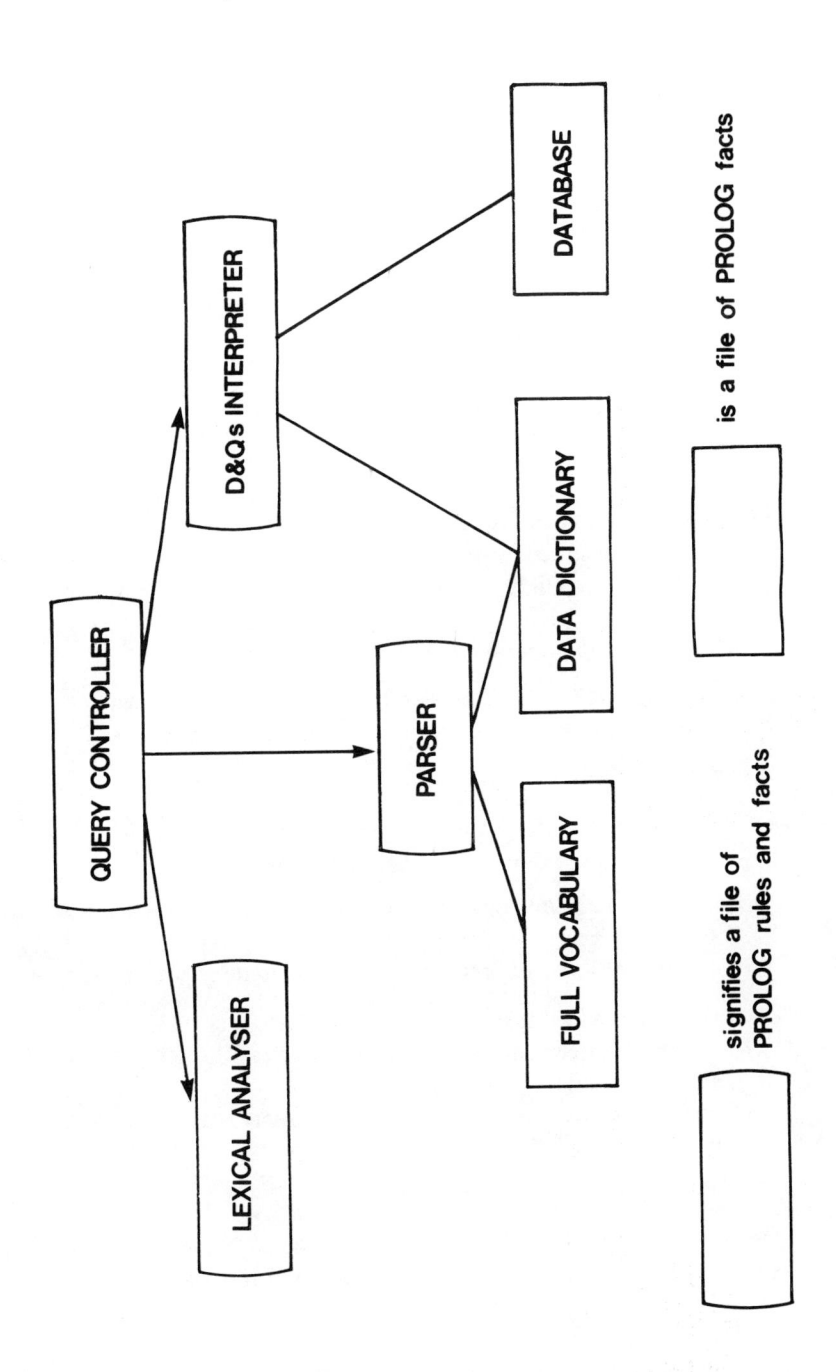

Fig. 6.2 – QPROC runtime components.

Only the files of facts (conventionally the "data") are application dependent. Thus the 'Query Controller', the 'Lexical Analyser', the 'D&Qs Interpreter' and even the 'Parser' run unchanged in every application.

The application independence is retained by writing a parser that recognises *linguistic* structures (such as noun phrases and verb phrases), but which uses the data dictionary dynamically to check the proposed parse and to help build the final interpretation.

3.4 The grammar
3.4.1

The grammar is founded on a set of context-free productions. For example, a noun phrase may begin with a determiner, followed by a number of adjectives, and end with a noun. This can be written:

    noun_phrase - -> determiner, adjectives, noun.
    adjectives   - -> true.
    adjectives   - -> adjective, adjectives.

A parser for such a grammar can be very easily written in PROLOG. (With many PROLOG systems such a parser is supplied in a standard library.) If the parser is given a set of productions like those above, and a sentence, it will answer 'yes' if the sentence is grammatical, and 'no' if it is not. This is rendered more useful if each non-terminal has a number of arguments, which form its 'augmentation'.

Thus every non-terminal can return its meaning:

    noun_phrase(Art,Adjs,Noun) - -> determiner(Det),
                                            adjectives(Adjs),
                                            noun(Noun).
    adjectives([ ]) - -> true
    adjectives([Adj | Adjs]) - -> adjective(Adj),
                                              adjectives(Adjs).

Now whenever a noun—phrase is successfully parsed it returns the determiner, 'Det', the list of adjectives, 'Adjs', and the noun, 'Noun'.

The grammar augmentation in QPROC is used for three purposes:

(1) to return the meaning of the non-terminal,
(2) to ensure agreement (for example between the subject and verb of the sentence),
(3) to pass on information gained from earlier parts of the sentence (or from the context) to help parse the rest.

3.4.2

QPROC's parser is written in an extension of PROLOG which is compiled into standard PROLOG by a grammar compiler [50]. For example,

    a - -> b, c

compiles into

> a(Input, Remainder) :— b(Input, Half_Way),
> c(Half_Way, Remainder).

The standard PROLOG requires two extra parameters recording the input to be parsed (in some suitable form) and the words "left over" — the 'Remainder'.

One other extension of particular interest is left recursion. A set of productions such as

> nph --> noun.
> nph --> nph, postmod.
> nph --> nph, postqual.

is naively compiled into

> nph(Input, Remainder) :—
>   noun(Input, Remainder).
> nph(Input, Remainder) :—
>   nph(Input, P2),
>   postmod(P2, Remainder).
> nph(Input, Remainder):—
>   nph(Input, P2),
>   postqual(P2, Remainder).

This unfortunately loops if it can not succeed.

Instead the grammar compiler detects left recursion and compiles the clauses into:

> nph(Input, Remainder) :—
>   noun(Input, P2),
>   recurse(nph, P2, Remainder).
> recurse(nph, P2, Remainder) :—
>   (postmod(P2, P3); postqual(P2,P3)),
>   recurse(nph, P3, Remainder).
> recurse(nph, Remainder, Remainder).

Thus a left recursive production is transformed into a tail recursion.

However, the example above is particularly simple. The grammar compiler must also deal with left recursive productions with augmentations:

> nph(Arg1, Arg2) --> noun(Arg1, Arg2).
> nph(Arg1, Arg3) --> nph(Arg1, Arg2), postmod(Arg2, Arg3).
> nph(Arg1, Arg2) --> nph(Arg1, Arg2), postqual.

In this case particular care has to be taken that the first argument, Arg1, appears unchanged on the original call to noun, but that the second argument (in this case Arg3) does not appear in the call to noun, because it may be affected by the recursion.

118 IMPLEMENTATION [Ch.

```
nph(Arg1, Arg3, Input, Remainder) :—
    noun(Arg1, Arg2, Input, P2),
    recurse(nph(Arg1, Arg2), nph(Arg1, Arg3), P2, Remainder).
recurse(nph(Arg1, Arg2), nph(Arg1, Arg3), P2, Remainder) :—
    postmod(Arg2, Intermediate, P2, P3),
    recurse(nph(Arg1, Intermediate), nph(Arg1, Arg3), P3, Remainder).
recurse(nph(Arg1, Arg2), nph(Arg1, Arg3), P2, Remainder) :—
    postqual(P2, P3),
    recurse(nph(Arg1, Arg2), nph(Arg1, Arg3), P3, Remainder).
recurse(nph(Arg1, Arg3), nph(Arg1, Arg3), Remainder, Remainder).
```

A problem which results from the compilation of left recursive grammar productions into tail-recursive PROLOG clauses is some loss of control of the order of evaluation. In practice the human grammar writer wants control over the order of the clauses for 'recurse' so that, for example, the parser may look for postmodifiers and when they have been found it exits, only searching for postqualifiers if driven by backtracking. QPROC's grammar compiler also provides for this kind of control.

3.4.3

Finally, let us look at an example of the interaction of syntax and semantics in QPROC's parser.

We consider the non-terminal 'noun/det' which parses the part of a noun phrase following the determiner and count:

(1) 'noun/det'(Adjs, Num&Case, Dom, Var, Core) - ->
(2)   forenouns(List),
(3)   word(noun,_,Num&Case, Headnoun),
(4)   test(qualify(List, Headnoun, Adjs, Dom, Var, Core)).
(5) qualify(List, entity(Ent), Adjs, domain(Ent), Var, [Ent, id=Var | Args]):—
(6)   quallist(List, Ent, Adjs, Args).

In the election application, the query

"Who contested the 1974 election?"

includes the noun phrase "the 1974 election". "1974 election" is parsed as a 'noun/det'.

'noun/det' returns a list of adjectives, 'Adjs', an ending 'Num&Case' which has the same form as endings in QPROC's vocabulary (see section 3.2 above).

It also returns 'Dom' which is the database entity or domain associated with the noun phrase. The value of Dom is used by the parser as a semantic check when slotting the noun phrase into the containing sentence. (Thus "Who has a seat?" is distinguished from "Who had 5000 votes?").

'Var' is the variable which will appear in the formal DESCRIPTION interpreting the noun phrase. 'Core' is the core QUALIFIER returned from the noun phrase. This is also used, in building up the DESCRIPTION (see Chapter 5, section 4.3).

When QPROC processes "the 1974 election" it calls 'noun/det' (line 1.) to deal with "1974 election". "1974" is parsed as a 'forenoun'. It is the only one, so 'forenouns' (line 2.) exits binding 'List', to

'[adj('1974', '=',domain(date))]'.

The next line,

word(noun,_,Num&Case,Headnoun)

requires a dictionary search to determine if the current word in the input sentence is a noun. 'Num&Case' is an ending and 'Headnoun' is a meaning, as described in section 3.2 above. For the word "election" the part of speech *is* 'noun', the ending is 'sing&_' and the meaning is 'entity(election)'. The attempt to match 'noun/det' has so far yielded the following unifications:

(1) 'noun/det'(Adjs, sing&Case, Dom, Var, Core) - ->
(2)   forenouns([adj('1974', '=',domain(date))]),
(3)   word(noun,_,sing&Case, entity(election)),
(4)   test(qualify([adj('1974', '=',domain(date))],
        entity(election),
        Adjs,
        Dom,
        Var,
        Core)).

On the right-hand side of a production, 'test(C)' as in

A - -> B, test (C), D

is a call to an ordinary PROLOG goal C.

At line 4 the PROLOG goal is

qualify([adj('1974','=',domain(date))], entity(election), Adjs, Dom, Var, Core)

for which the matching clause is at lines 5 & 6.

quallist([adj('1974','=',domain(date))], election, Adjs, Args)

'quallist' looks up the data definition for election and finds that the attribute 'date' ranges over the domain 'date'. It then binds 'Adjs' to the singleton [adjs('1974', V)]', and 'Args' to the singleton [date = V].

Thus line 4 exits as

test(qualify([adj('1974','=',domain(date))],
                entity(election),
                [adjs('1974',V)],
                election,
                Var,
                [election,id=Var,date=V]))

and 'noun/det' exits as:

'noun/det'([adjs('1974',V)],
             sing&Case,
             election,
             Var,
             [election,id=Var,date=V]).

7

Current developments in natural language access to databases

1. INTRODUCTION

A good guide to recent developments in natural language front ends is the Proceedings of the Conference on Applied Natural Language Processing, Santa Monica, California, February 1983. A number of systems are being developed in languages other than English, most notably the PLIDIS system [2], for German. The PROLOG language was initially conceived for writing natural language parsers in France and developments still continue in that country. Japan also has a special interest in the development of speech understanding systems because they have three different alphabets which adds considerably to the problem of understanding written Japanese! However, to keep abreast of developments in natural language understanding, the *American Journal of Computational Linguistics* still remains the best single source of up to date information. For readers wishing to get a more thorough grasp of computational analysis of natural language, Winograd [57] provides a very complete and well-written text.

2. CURRENT SYSTEMS

The first natural language (NL) front ends are already on the market. Ahead of the field is Artificial Intelligence Corporation's INTELLECT which has been available for over three years, but every day new products are advertised and a recent survey of commercial database systems in *Computer News* (2nd February 1984) credited four of them with "fifth generation" "lexion driven" languages.

The current commercially available systems are tied to specific, fairly restricted, formal query languages. There is no attempt to get at the meaning of the natural language input, but rather to construct a formal query which includes everything mentioned by the user. Such a system can very rarely recognise if the user's intended meaning is beyond the scope of its formal query language.

One of the most essential components of an NL system is the facility to refer back to previous queries, and current systems can usually deal with pronouns at least.

The style of algorithm used to interpret pronouns is that

(1) a pronoun refers back to the result specification and rule of the previous query, or
(2) if the rule from the previous query is inconsistent with the rule from the current query, the pronoun refers back to the result specification without the rule (or perhaps to the query before last).

For example

"Give the name and current balance for customers in Berks"
→ LIST CUSTOMER.NAME, BALANCE WHERE
   CUSTOMER.COUNTY = 'BERKSHIRE'
"List their orders"
→ LIST CUSTOMER.NAME, BALANCE, ORDER.ORDERCODE
   WHERE ORDER.CUSTOMER = CUSTOMER.CODE AND
   CUSTOMER.COUNTY = 'BERKSHIRE'

Current systems are generally tailored for an application by an initial installation and then improved by trial and error. The initial installation involves extracting relation names, values, etc. from the new database (either automatically or by hand) and adding them to the built-in natural language vocabulary (which has words like 'and', 'print' etc.). The improvement by trial and error occurs when a log of users' interactions with the system is examined (or when users complain!) and new synonyms are added to the vocabulary. Sometimes the installation of an NL front end brings out errors in the database design itself. For example if a personal database includes an employee's salary history in the same record as his current details, any query like "list employees with salary under £7,000" will yield the wrong answer since it will include any employee who has ever had a salary under £7,000. Thus installing a natural language front end may require a normalisation process to be carried out on the database.

3. MAPPING NATURAL LANGUAGE ONTO CURRENT DATABASES

In order to put an NL front end on an existing database, the natural language vocabulary must be tailored to the application, and the formal queries generated by the front end must be tailored for the DBMS.

Each NL front end is built around a set of data modelling concepts. Every word in the vocabulary must map onto a data item in this set. Typically a front end will map words onto entity names, relationships, attribute names and attribute values. This set may be augmented by special "goodies" like entity identifiers or selection expressions.

In order to tailor the NL front end to a DBMS it is therefore necessary to map the NL's data modelling concepts onto the data model of the DBMS.

To map entities and relationships onto the relational model, for example, we can map entities onto relations and relationships onto joins between the relations. In Chapter 5, section 3, I mentioned 'implicit' joins, where the attributes used in the join formed an identifier for one of the relations. A useful rule is to map relationships only onto implicit joins, in order to avoid generating from a natural language enquiry alternative formal queries which could not represent the intended meaning.

For example, to interpret "list employees on project X" an NL front end might seek entities called EMPLOYEE and PROJECT and a relationship between them.

Suppose the relation database included relations

Relation	Attribute	
EMPLOYEE	CODE	
EMPLOYEE	ADDRESS	(home address)
EMPLOYEE	PROJECT	
PROJECT	CODE	
PROJECT	LOCATION	

then the sole relationship defined between them should map onto

EMPLOYEE.PROJECT = PROJECT.CODE.

If another relationship was defined between them mapping onto

EMPLOYEE.ADDRESS = PROJECT.LOCATION

then the query "list employees on project X" would yield two interpretations, the second have the incorrect meaning "list employees whose home address is the same of the location of project X".

To map entities and relationship onto the CODASYL data model on the other hand, we can map entities onto records, and relationships onto sets.

Once a mapping has been defined from the NL front end's data model onto that of the DBMS, it remains to determine how the formal queries output by the front end should be executed against the database. The simplest method is simply to translate the NL front end's output formal queries into a formal query language that has already been implemented on the DBMS. A possibly more efficient method is to provide an interpreter which directly evaluates the NL front end's formal output queries by making low level calls on the database.

4. DEVELOPMENTS

Now that more and more users are able to try out natural language interfaces, the priorities for future development can be assigned in the light of hands-on experience.

4.1 Metaquestions

First of all users want to ask not just about the data in the database, but explanatory questions about what the database itself contains. For example, a user coming to a personnel database for the first time might want to ask "What information do you have on employees?", "Do you know the distance between company locations?" and so on. Such 'metaquestions' are quite hard to distinguish from database questions, because a database question may be phrased in much the same way as a metaquestion.

    Q "What is there on employees?" ⟨Metaquestion⟩
    A "Personnel no., date of birth, data of joining, grade, salary, department"

    Q "What is there in bin 01?" ⟨Data question⟩
    A "Pencils and pens"

A short-cut to processing metaqueries is to associate explanatory text with certain keywords. Thus any query including such a keyword is treated as a metaquery. Typical keywords are "help" and "file", so for example "What is in the employee *file*?" is treated as a metaquery. This approach will not necessarily work for queries like "What is there on employees?"

    The second way around the problem is to present a pictorial representation of the database so that the user can refer to it before asking his question. It was the facility to represent the word on the screen which made Winograd's SHRDLU so compelling. Clearly this approach is impracticable for complex databases.

4.2 Vertical NL systems

When an NL front end is tailored to a database its built-in vocabulary is augmented by the database names, and further tailoring requires an expert to define all the synonyms which end users could employ in natural language queries.

    A way to short-cut the second step is to produce a 'vertical' system for each application. Whereas an NL front end is usually designed to be transportable between applications, a 'vertical' system is designed for a specific application and it may include the database as well as the NL front end. A vertical natural language system for a personnel application would include all synonyms for "employee" ("worker", "hand", "staff"), "salary" ("remuneration", "pay", "wage") etc. Such a system can be tailored to a database by merely mapping one word from each set of synonyms onto the database. For more complex, or less well defined, applications vertical systems are very difficult to design.

4.3 Database update
Current NL front ends concentrate on database enquiry. Clearly an important step forward would be to provide NL update but this presupposes a solution to the problem of data integrity. The classic problem is the update "Change Smith's manager to Goodman" on a database which associated managers with *departments* and not *employees*. Should Smith's department be changed to that managed by Goodman, or should the manager be changed to Goodman for the department currently associated with Smith? For this example one could envisage a simple dialogue enabling the end user to select his intended command. In general, however, the constraints may be quite complex and it may be difficult to generate an appropriate dialogue without dropping into the jargon of databases.

4.4 Learning new natural language words and expressions
Many current systems offer a facility for the end user to define his own synonyms or paraphrases. If a system can be taught by the user in this way, problems may arise if several different users define synonyms which interact with each other (e.g. if one user defines "pr" as "product" and another defines it as "printer"). On the other hand, there are practical drawbacks in giving each user a private vocabulary — this could mean all users would have to be specially "introduced" to the NL front end before they could use it.

4.5 Major extensions
The system described in this book uses a logical meaning representation to record its understanding of the natural language enquiry before translating this into a formal database query. It also evaluates definite noun phrases to determine their reference separately from the remainder of the query. The move towards an NL system whose understanding covers anything expressible in logic is a major step forward, and the limits of what is expressible in logic are continually expanding. In addition to the traditional logical concepts of the predicate calculus, further concepts such as presupposition, events, time and approximate reasoning are being absorbed into a unified formalism.

Even the apparently simple logical operator 'not' is hard to implement on live databases, and it will be some time before the extended logic described here is available through formal query languages. However, the facility to interpret natural language into a logical representation more powerful than the underlying query language is still important to avoid translating an NL query into something the user did not mean. Such a front end can instead tell the user that the underlying data system cannot answer his request. An even better front end will actually translate a single logical structure into a number of separate database queries which ultimately yield the required answers.

The second major extension is to program the NL front end to use language as a way of achieving a conversational goal (satisfying the user's requirements) rather than simply to understand questions and statements. Such a front end takes the user's natural language query as a starting point in a chain of reasoning which attempts to assess what the user really meant and what he might have asked had he known a bit more about the database.

Finally, there is an obvious need to connect an NL front end to a range of software to enhance the man—machine interface and to augment the database access component.

For user input the extra software will enable the user to point to objects as well as naming them. Natural language may well be used to augment menu systems for certain applications. In the longer term NL front ends may be integrated with voice recognition software to produce a single module which will "understand", at some level, spoken language.

For user output, NL systems such as INTELLECT are already being integrated with graphics packages. Thus instead of results being output as a table they can be expressed as a pie chart or histogram. Of course natural language generation is a necessary part of an NL front end, but in current systems the NL output is very simple. Surprisingly NL input and NL generation are really quite distinct tasks and it is possible that separate NL generation packages will be grafted onto NL front ends in the future.

For database access a number of enhancements can be made by utilising other software. The most immediate application is for statistical processing of the data. (INTELLECT again offers an interface to such packages, indicated in the natural language input by a single keyword which indicates the required processing). In the longer term the database access component will be augmented by a reasoning system which will be able to deduce answers from the given data. (In a current laboratory system this component deduces the distance between two ships from their current positions, and works out how long it will take them to rendezvous from their respective cruising speeds.)

5. NETWORKING

Current natural language systems run on centralised database systems maintained by a support team. An end user of a natural language front end uses standard terminals through which he generally has to log in to the operating system and call up the NL enquiry system, before starting to use natural language.

Clearly the near future will see terminals directly connected to specific programs, and NL enquiry will be a prime candidate. Thus the terminal in the personnel manager's office will automatically connect to an NL front end for the personnel database as soon as he switches on and types his password.

Another development already in hand is to put an NL front end onto an intelligent terminal, so that the NL analysis is done at the terminal and only the database calls are passed up the line to the mainframe computer. An important prerequisite for this type of facility is that the NL system must be able to make sensible guesses at the meaning of unknown words. Such words are likely to represent data values occurring in the database, but it would be impossible to store all such words in a vocabulary on the terminal, and inappropriate to send a special search command to the mainframe to confirm the appearance in the database of each unknown word.

The final development will be the introduction of complete natural language database systems which will run on a microcomputer. These will be used for personal databases created, updated and maintained by the end user. Surprisingly, perhaps, these are in many ways easier to build than natural language front ends because the database structures are designed to support the exact meaning representations generated by the NL analyser.

The systems currently in existence (e.g. [48]) work on binary relations and allow the user to define new relations by a simple dialogue

Q "Create the attribute : colour"
A "The attribute colour has been added"

Q "Individuals : white, blue, black, grey"
A "The following individuals have been added:
white blue black grey"

When a manager has a personal NL database system on his own microcomputer, he will be able to add information to the database using natural language. Although entered randomly the system will be able to retrieve the data sorted and correlated in any way he wants by merely expressing his requirements in his natural language.

Appendix 1

A pilot implementation

This book has described the architecture of a natural language enquiry system. The development of the design was continually checked by programming, and the practical result was a pilot QPROC system that implemented most of the designed features. The pilot system lacked:

(1) any implementation of *context*,
(2) comparisons, other than "=".

However, it served well to demonstrate the possibilities of QPROC and was adapted to three databases: an expanded version of the election database, the COPSE database and an *archery* database designed by W. Pitkin. The system was written completely in the PROLOG language, and it included four modules.

DCG: This was a major extension and adaptation of PROLOG's "definite clause grammar" implementation [50].
SYNTAX: This was a parser which dynamically accessed the data dictionary of the attached database (election, COPSE or archery).
DIC: This was a core dictionary in the form of PROLOG facts.
EX: This was a program that executed the formal queries, which were expressed in the language of D&Qs, on a PROLOG database.

Examples
This demonstration exhibits queries to the election database, and the answers actually returned by the pilot version of QPROC. The numbered queries were entered by a user, and the answers he obtained are shown indented. The examples are divided into 9 groups to illustrate different features of QPROC.

1. Focus
   The focus of a question is the thing we want to know. We often indicate the focus with a question word such as "what" or "how".

   Questions.
   1.1 How old is Mrs Smith?
       37
   1.2 Smith is what age?
       37
   1.3 Whose title is 'Prof'?
       Barron

2. Adjectives
   We use adjectives before a noun to restrict the set of things it can refer to.

   Questions.
   2.1 Name a London constituency.
       Newham
   2.2 List the tory candidates.
       2 were found:
           Smith Disraeli

3. The verb to "be"
   This is very common. It can be used between a thing and its properties (as in 3.1), or between 2 sets of things (as in 3.2).

   Questions.
   3.1 Who is liberal?
       2 were found:
           Gladstone Barron
   3.2 Which constituencies are Smith and Barron members for?
       Smith: Worthing
       Barron: Southampton

4. Templates
   Other verbs expect a range of verb modifiers. For example "at Worthing", in 4.1, defines the location of the action. The verb modifiers can occur before the verb, as in 4.2 as well as after. The preposition can even be split from its noun phrase, as in 4.3.

   Questions.
   4.1 Who stood at Worthing for the Labour party in 1974?
       Jones
   4.2 In what year did Disraeli stand?
       1975
   4.3 What did Smith win by?
       3000

5. Question words
   The specific question word tells QPROC what sort of answer is required. "When" refers to a *date,* "where" to a *place,* etc.

   Questions.
   5.1 Smith won what, when, where?
       elect1
       elect1: 1974
       1974 and elect1: Worthing
   5.2 Who lost to who at Worthing?
       2 were found:
           Jones Gladstone
       Jones: Smith
       Gladstone: Smith

6. Noun modifiers
   Nouns as well as verbs can be qualified by prepositional phrases. Translating this into formal queries requires intelligent use of the data dictionary.

   In 6.1 "candidate" is a relation, and the sentence is a paraphrase of "Who were the labour candidates?".

   In 6.2, the system recognises that there were different elections in 1974 and 1975 and gives the location of each.

   Finally in 6.3, a path is found from a party ("SDP") to a candidate, to an election, to a constituency ("Newham").

   Questions.
   6.1 Who were the candidates for the labour party?
       2 were found:
           Jones Freeston
   6.2 Where were the elections in 1974 and 1975?
       elect1: Worthing
       elect2: Newham
   6.3 Who was the Social Democrat at Southampton?
       Robson

7. Relative clauses
   A relative clause is a sentence with a variable in it, (e.g. 7.1 "... who contested Worthing"). This acts as a qualification on the head noun ("candidates"). The variable in a relative clause may be the subject of the clause as in 7.1, or an element of the template (e.g. in 7.2 it is the *location:* "... in which Heath stood"). Notice that in 7.3 the relative clause qualifies the immediately preceding noun, but in 7.4 it qualifies an earlier noun. The relative pronoun "who" can only stand for *people* and not for constituencies.

Questions.
7.1 List the candidates who contested Worthing.
   3 were found:
      Smith Jones Gladstone
7.2 What is the area of the constituency in which Heath stood?
   London
7.3 Give a seat whose member is liberal.
   Southampton
7.4 Name the member in a southern constituency who is 50!
   Barron

8. Determiners
A definite noun phrase is supposed to have a unique reference. Because there was more than one election at Southampton, the *singular definite* noun phrase "the election at Southampton" does not refer, and so it yields an error. A noun phrase without a determiner (8.3 – "2 elections") is, by default, an *indefinite* noun phrase.

Questions.
8.1 Who stood in the election at Southampton?
   The computer cannot understand what "the election at Southampton" refers to.
8.2 Who stood in an election at Southampton?
   3 were found:
      Freeston Robson Barron
8.3 Who stood in 2 elections?
   Jones

9. Misleading sentences
Certain ambiguities have to be cleared up by the data dictionary.

In 9.1 the number "2" counts the size of the set referred to by the noun phrase. In 9.2, on the other hand, "1" is merely an adjective before "vote".

In 9.3 "is" is the main verb, but in 9.4 "was" is an 'auxiliary' verb which comes before the subject.

In 9.5 the prepositional phrase, "to Smith", is a verb modifier for the verb, "lost".

In 9.6 the prepositional phrase "in London" modifies the noun, "an election".

Questions.
9.1 Who stood in 2 elections?
   Jones

9.2 Who won by 1 vote?
     Robson
9.3 Where is Newham?
     London
9.4 Where was Smith standing?
     Worthing
9.5 Who lost an election to Smith?
     2 were found:
         Jones Gladstone
9.6 Who lost an election in London?
     Disraeli

10. Unrecognised words and symbols
    QPROC ignores unexpected punctuation and words it cannot recognise. This is signalled to the user by a series of question marks underneath the word. This facility enables QPROC to deal with various colourfully worded queries successfully.

    Questions.
    10.1 Who is a PASCAL-loving professor around here???
              ???????? ??????   ??????????
          Barron

Appendix 2

Specification of D&Qs

1. SYNTAX

LHS ::− RHS	The left-hand side is defined by the right-hand side.
⟨Non Terminal⟩	On the RHS, non-terminals are put in angled brackets.
A | B	An 'A' or a 'B' may occur here on the RHS.
A { B | C } D	This is an 'A' on the RHS followed by a 'B' or 'C', then a 'D'.
nil	Nothing

The full syntax of D&Qs is:

QUALIFIER ::− ⟨PREDICATE⟩ | ⟨PREDICATE⟩(⟨SELECTIONS⟩).
QUALIFIER ::− ⟨QUALIFIER⟩ { & | or } ⟨QUALIFIER⟩ | not ⟨QUALIFIER⟩.
QUALIFIER ::− ⟨DESCRIPTION⟩ is qual(⟨VARIABLE⟩, ⟨QUALIFIER⟩).
QUALIFIER ::− true | fail.

DESCRIPTION ::− ⟨CONSTANT⟩.
DESCRIPTION ::− ⟨DETERMINER⟩-⟨COUNT⟩-qual(⟨VARIABLE⟩, ⟨QUALIFIER⟩).
DESCRIPTION ::− ⟨DESCRIPTION⟩ is funct(⟨VARIABLE⟩, ⟨DESCRIPTION⟩).
DESCRIPTION ::− ⟨DESCRIPTION⟩ { & | or } ⟨DESCRIPTION⟩.

SELECTIONS ::− ⟨ATTRIBUTE⟩ ⟨COMPARISON⟩ ⟨VARIABLE⟩ { , ⟨SELECTIONS⟩ | nil }.

COMPARISON ::− = | ≠ | < | > | ≤ | ≥.
DETERMINER ::− the | any | what.
COUNT ::− ⟨INTEGER⟩ | ⟨VARIABLE⟩.

CONSTANT   is a PROLOG atom or integer.
INTEGER   is a PROLOG integer.
PREDICATE   is a PROLOG atom.
ATTRIBUTE   is a PROLOG atom.
VARIABLE   is a PROLOG variable.

Given certain operator declarations, each D&Qs formula becomes a PROLOG structure.

'not' must be declared as a prefix operator.
'&', 'or' must be declared as infix operators.

2. FORMALISM

This appendix gives the semantics of D&Qs.
The semantics comprises

Satisfaction of DESCRIPTIONS and QUALIFIERS
Reference of DESCRIPTIONS
Results of DESCRIPTIONS and QUALIFIERS

Before launching into the specifications of these three components of meaning, a formalism is introduced which will keep the definitions short and meaningful.

$Q\{X_1, X_2, \ldots X_n\}$ represents a formula whose free variables are $X_1, X_2, \ldots X_n$.

$X_1 \equiv G_1, X_2 \equiv G_2, \ldots, X_n \equiv G_n$ represents an association set.

$Q\{G_1/X_1, G_2/X_2, \ldots G_n/X_n\}$ represents the substituted formula which results from substituting the group (i.e. set, bag or list) of constants, G_i, for each free occurrence of the variable, X_i, in the formula Q.

X represents the group $X_1, X_2, \ldots X_n$ with n unspecified.
$Q\{\mathbf{X}\}$ represents $Q\{X_1, X_2, \ldots X_n\}$
$\mathbf{X} \equiv \mathbf{G}$ represents $X_1 \equiv G_1, X_2 \equiv G_2, \ldots X_n \equiv G_n$
$Q\{\mathbf{G}/\mathbf{X}\}$ represents $Q\{G_1/X_1, G_2/X_2, \ldots G_n/X_n\}$

$\mathbf{X} \equiv \mathbf{G_X}$ and $\mathbf{Y} \equiv \mathbf{G_Y}$ are 'compatible' if the variables which occur in both association sets have the same association in each set. The "same association" is defined by equality of groups (Chapter 4, section 2.1).

The union of two compatible association sets, $\mathbf{X} \equiv \mathbf{G_X}$ and $\mathbf{Y} \equiv \mathbf{G_Y}$ is written

'$\mathbf{X} \equiv \mathbf{G_X}$ union $\mathbf{Y} \equiv \mathbf{G_Y}$'

3. SPECIFICATION OF SEMANTICS

3.1 Satisfaction of simple QUALIFIERS

The concept of "satisfaction" is inherited from the predicate calculus. The concept depends upon the notion of a "free" variable, which can briefly be defined.

Any variable, V, occurring in a simple QUALIFIER, Relation(..., Attribute @ V, ...) (where '@' is a comparison) is free.

If V is free in QUALIFIER Q1, then it is free in 'not Q1', 'Q1 & Q2', 'Q1 or Q2', 'Q2 & Q1', 'Q2 or Q1'.

If V is free in DESCRIPTION D1, then it is free in 'D1 & D2', 'D1 or D2', 'D2 & D1', 'D2 or D1'.

If V is different from X and V is free in QUALIFIER Q, then V is free in 'D is qual(X,Q)' and 'Det-N-qual(X,Q)'.

Finally if V is different from X, and V is free in D1 then V is free in 'D2 is funct(X,D1)'.

A formula is satisfied, in general, by an "association set" which associates a group (i.e. set, bag or list) with each of its free variables. If a formula has no free variables it is satisfied (by the empty association set) if it succeeds against the given database. We say, in this case, that it is "true". If a formula with no free variables is not true it is "false".

A simple qualifier Q with free variables $V_1, V_2, \ldots V_n$ is satisfied by the association set $V_1 \equiv G_1, V_2 \equiv G_2, \ldots V_n \equiv G_n$ if the QUALIFIER, 'Q{$G_1/V_1, G_2/V_2, \ldots G_n/V_n$}', with no free variables, which results from Q by substituting G_i for all occurrences of V_i (i=1, ... n), is true.

$$\text{rel}(att_1 \ @_1 \ G_1, att_2 \ @_2 \ G_2, \ldots)$$

is a simple QUALIFIER with no free variables.

(1) If there are no selection expressions, so the simple QUALIFIER has the form 'rel', then it is true if and only if the relation 'rel' is non-empty.
(2) If att_1 has 'atom type' (see Chapter 4, section 2.1)
   (a) G_1 is a set with elements $c_1, c_2, \ldots c_n$ or G_1 is an atom, c_1,
   (b) rel_i is a non-empty derived relation containing all and only those tuples of 'rel' which satisfy '$att_1 \ @_1 \ c_i$' for i = 1, ... n (or i = 1),
   (c) each '$rel_i(att_2 \ @_2 \ G_2, \ldots)$' is true.
(3) If att_1 has 'set type':
   (a) G_1 is a set with subsets $G_{11}, \ldots G_{1n}$ whose union is G_1,
   (b) rel_i is a non-empty derived relation containing all and only those tuples of 'rel' which satisfy '$att_1 \ @_1 \ G_{1i}$'. (Unless the comparison '$@_1$' is defined on sets, '$att_1 \ @_1 \ G_{1i}$' is meaningless. Semantically, therefore, the QUALIFIER is well-defined only if '$@_1$' is '=').
   (c) each '$rel_i(att_2 \ @_2 \ G_2, \ldots)$' is true.

(4) If att$_1$ has 'bag type':
  (a) G_1 is a bag and $G_{11}, G_{12}, \ldots G_{1n}$ are bags whose union (as defined in Chapter 4, section 2.1) is G_1,
  (b) as for 3(b),
  (c) as for 3(c).
(5) If att$_1$ has 'list type':
  (a) G_1 is a list which results from appending $G_{11}, G_{12}, \ldots G_{1n}$,
  (b) as for 3(b),
  (c) as for 3(c).

3.2 Satisfaction of Curried QUALIFIERS

A Curried QUALIFIER has the form 'qual(V,Qual)' where 'Qual' is a QUALIFIER, and 'V' is a variable. It is satisfied by $X \equiv G_X$ and 'returns' the group G_V if 'Qual' is satisfied by

$$V \equiv G_1, \quad X \equiv G_X,$$
$$\text{and by} \quad V \equiv G_2, \quad X \equiv G_X,$$
$$\text{and by} \quad \ldots,$$
$$\text{and by} \quad V \equiv G_n, \quad X \equiv G_X$$

where G_V is the union of $G_1, G_2, \ldots G_n$.

If Qual is the simple QUALIFIER 'person(name=X,age>Y)', then 'qual(Y, person(name=X,age>Y))' is satisfied by $X \equiv$ ['SMITH', 'JONES'] and returns the set [50] only if 'person(name=X,age>Y)' is satisfied by

$$X \equiv \text{['SMITH', 'JONES']}, Y \equiv [50].$$

If Qual is any *simple* QUALIFIER, with free variable V, the 'qual(V,Qual)' is satisfied by $X \equiv G_X$ and returns G_V only if Qual is satisfied by $V \equiv G_V, X \equiv G_X$.

However, if Qual is a QUALIFIER such as 'Desc is qual(V$_2$,Qual$_2$)', where 'Desc' is a DESCRIPTION and 'qual(V$_2$,Qual$_2$)' another Curried QUALIFIER then the above equivalence does not necessarily hold. A counter-example will be given in section 3.4.

If V is not free in Qual, the 'qual(V,Qual)' is satisfied by $X \equiv G_X$ and returns any group if Qual is satisfied by the same association set.

3.3 The reference of a DESCRIPTION

3.3.1 Simple DESCRIPTIONS

A Curried QUALIFIER can return either a set, a bag or a list. The reference of a DESCRIPTION on the other hand may only be a bag or a list.

3.3.2 Compound DESCRIPTIONS

A compound DESCRIPTION has the form 'Determiner-Number-qual(V,Qual)'. If 'qual(V,Qual)' is satisfied by $X \equiv G_X$ and returns the group G_V with more than N elements, then the DESCRIPTION 'Det-N-qual(V,Qual)' is also satisfied, with the same association set. If the group G_V is a bag or a list then this is its reference. If G_V is a set, however, then the reference is a bag containing each of the elements of G_V only once.

Thus "2 people", 'Det-2-qual(V,person(name=V))' is satisfied by the empty association set. It refers to the bag ['SMITH', 'JONES'] if 'person(name=V)' is satisfied by V≡['SMITH','JONES'].

3.3.3 Disjunctive DESCRIPTIONS

A disjunctive DESCRIPTION has the form 'Desc$_1$ or Desc$_2$'. If Desc$_1$ has free variables X, and Desc$_2$ has free variables Y, then 'Desc$_1$ or Desc$_2$' is satisfied by '**X**≡**G$_X$** union **Y**≡**G$_Y$**' and refers to the group G if:

(1) **X**≡**G$_X$** and **Y**≡**G$_Y$** are compatible,
(2) Desc$_1$ is satisfied by **X**≡**G$_X$** and refers to G (in which case G_Y is any group), or Desc$_2$ is satisfied by **Y**≡**G$_Y$** and refers to G (in which case G_X is any group).

3.3.4 Conjunctive DESCRIPTIONS

A conjunctive DESCRIPTION has the form 'Desc$_1$ & Desc$_2$'. It is satisfied by '**X**≡**G$_X$** union **Y**≡**G$_Y$**' if Desc$_1$ is satisfied by **X**≡**G$_X$**, Desc$_2$ is satisfied by a compatible association list **Y**≡**G$_Y$**. Its reference is the union of the two groups referred to by Desc$_1$ and Desc$_2$.

3.3.5 Natural language functions

A natural language function has the form 'Desc$_1$ is funct(V,Desc$_2$)'. It is satisfied by '**X**≡**G$_X$** union **Y**≡**G$_Y$**' if

(1) Desc$_1$ is satisfied by **X**≡**G$_X$** and refers to G,
(2) there exist groups $G_1, \ldots G_n$ (generally each G_i is a singleton) whose union is G,
(3) Desc$_2$ is satisfied by '**V**≡**G$_{Vi}$** union **Y**≡**G$_Y$**' and refers to Ref$_i$ for each $i=1,\ldots n$,
(4) each of the pairs G_i and G_{Vi} are equal groups (by the definition in Chapter 4, section 2.1).

The reference of 'Desc$_1$ is funct(V,Desc$_2$)' may be a bag or list depending which the reference of Desc$_1$ is.

If Desc$_1$ refers to a bag then the reference of the whole natural language function 'Desc$_1$ is funct(V,Desc$_2$)', is 'Ref$_1$ union Ref$_2$ ... union Ref$_n$', where these are defined above.

If Desc$_1$ refers to a list, then each of the Ref$_i$ must be converted into a list, L_i. (If Ref$_i$ is a list itself, or a singleton, then L_i=Ref$_i$. Otherwise L_i results from Ref$_i$ by imposing an arbitrary ordering on it.) The whole reference of the natural language function, 'Desc$_1$ is funct(V,Desc$_2$)', is the list, 'L_1 union L_2 ... union L_n'.

3.3.6 Example of a natural language function
This is all best illustrated by an example,

"The orders for which two Berkshire customers".

The DESCRIPTION corresponding to Desc$_1$ is,

what-2-qual(X, customer(name=X, region='berkshire'))
". . . which two Berkshire customers"

The function 'funct(V, Desc$_2$)' becomes,

funct(V, the-N-qual(Y, order(code=Y, customer=V)))
"The orders for ⟨customer V⟩"

The relevant relations are:

customer	name	region	...
	'Good Co'	'berkshire'	...
	'Better Co'	'avon'	...
	'Best Co'	'berkshire'	...
	...	...	...

order	code	customer	...
	01	'Good Co'	...
	02	'Good Co'	...
	03	'Better Co'	...
	04	'Best Co'	...
	...	...	...

The whole natural language function is,

what-2-qual(X, customer(name=X, region='berkshire'))
is funct(V, the-N-qual(Y, order(code=Y, customer=V))).

This is satisfied by the empty association set because:

(1) 'what-2-qual(X, customer(name=X, region='berkshire'))' is satisfied by the empty association set and refers to the bag ['Good Co', 'Best Co'],
(2) this bag is the union of two singleton bags, ['Good Co'] and ['Best Co'],
(3) 'the-N-qual(Y, order(code=Y, customer=V))' is satisfied by V ≡ ['Good Co'] and refers to the bag [01,02], and it is satisfied by V ≡ ['Best Co'] and refers to the bag [04] (in evaluating the natural language function it is irrelevant that this DESCRIPTION is also satisfied by V ≡ ['Better Co']),
(4) the set ['Good Co'] which satisfied V in (3) above is equal to the bag ['Good Co'] mentioned in (2) above. Similarly the set ['Best Co'] is equal to the bag ['Best Co.],
(5) the reference of the natural language function is '[01,02] union [04]' which is written [01,02,04].

3.4 Compound QUALIFIERS

A compound QUALIFIER has the form 'Desc is qual(V,Qual)' where Desc is a DESCRIPTION and Qual is a QUALIFIER. This is satisfied by $X \equiv G_X$ union $Y \equiv G_Y$ if,

(1) Desc is satisfied by $X \equiv G_X$ and refers to Ref,
(2) the Curried QUALIFIER 'qual(V,Qual)' is satisfied by $Y \equiv G_Y$ which is compatible with $X \equiv G_X$ and returns G,
(3) Ref and G are equal.

Thus, using the example from natural language functions, 'berkshire' is qual(X, customer(name=Y, region=X)) is satisfied by X ≡ ['Good Co', 'Best Co'] because

(1) 'berkshire' is satisfied by the empty association set and refers to the bag ['berkshire'],
(2) qual(X,customer(name=Y, region=X)) is satisfied by Y ≡ ['Good Co','Best Co'] (incidentally it is also satisfied by Y ≡ ['Better Co'] returning the set ['avon'], but this is irrelevant for the whole Curried qualifier),
(3) the bag ['berkshire'] and the set ['berkshire'] are equal.

We are now in a position to display a Curried QUALIFIER, 'qual(V,Qual)', which is satisfied by an association set $X \equiv G_X$ and returns a set G, although Qual is not itself satisfied by $X \equiv G_X$ union $V \equiv G$. The required formula is

'qual(V, any-N-qual(X1,true) is qual(X2, customer(name=V, region=X2)))'

This formula has no free variables, so it is satisfied by the empty association set. It returns the set ['Good Co','Better Co','Best Co'] because:

(1) 'qual(X2, customer(name=V, region=X2))'
is satisfied by V ≡ ['Better Co'] returning the set ['avon'], and by V ≡ ['Good Co', 'Best Co'] returning the set ['berkshire'],
(2) 'any-N-qual(X1,true)' is the trivial DESCRIPTION which is refers to any non-empty group; in particular it may refer to the bag ['avon'], or the bag ['berkshire'],
(3) 'any-N-qual(X1,true) is qual(X2, customer(name=V, region=X2))' is thus satisfied by V ≡ ['Better Co'], and by V ≡ ['Good Co', 'Best Co'],
(4) checking back to the definition of satisfaction of compound QUALIFIERS we see that,

'qual(V, any-N-qual(X1,true) is qual(X2, customer(name=V, region=X2)))'

returns the set ['Good Co','Better Co','Best Co'] (in any order).

3.5 Logical combination of QUALIFIERS

3.5.1 Conjunctive QUALIFIERS

A conjunctive QUALIFIER has the form 'Qual$_1$ & Qual$_2$' where Qual$_1$ and Qual$_2$ are QUALIFIERs. If Qual$_1$ and Qual$_2$ are satisfied by compatible association sets $V_1 \equiv G_1$ and $V_1 \equiv G_2$ then 'Qual$_1$ & Qual$_2$' is satisfied by $V_1 \equiv G_1$ union $V_2 \equiv G_2$.

3.5.2 Disjunctive QUALIFIERS

A disjunctive QUALIFIER has the form 'Qual$_1$ or Qual$_2$'. If V_1 is the set of free variables in Qual$_1$, and V_2 is the set of free variables in Qual$_2$, then 'Qual$_1$ or Qual$_2$' is satisfied by $V_1 \equiv G_1$ union $V_2 \equiv G_2$ under these circumstances:
(1) $V_1 \equiv G_1$ and $V_2 \equiv G_2$ are compatible association sets,
(2) Qual$_1$ is satisfied by $V_1 \equiv G_1$ (in which case G_2 is any group) or Qual$_2$ is satisfied by $V_2 \equiv G_2$ (in which case G_1 is any group).

3.5.3 Negated QUALIFIERS

A negated QUALIFIER has the form 'not Qual'. If $V_1, V_2, \ldots V_n$ is the set of free variables in Qual, then 'not Qual' is satisfied by $V_1 \equiv G_1, V_2 \equiv G_2, \ldots V_n \equiv G_n$ unless there exist subsets $S_1, S_2, \ldots S_n$ of $G_1, G_2, \ldots G_n$ such that Qual is satisfied by $V_1 \equiv S_1, V_2 \equiv S_2, \ldots V_n \equiv S_n$.

This completes the specification of "satisfaction" for D&Qs formulae.

3.6 Results

3.6.1 Preliminary definitions

[ ] is the empty result.

Res$_1$ union Res$_2$ is defined by two clauses:

> [Res$_{A1}$ + Res$_{A2}$] union [Res$_{B1}$ + Res$_{B2}$] is defined as
> [(Res$_{A1}$ union Res$_{B1}$) + (Res$_{A2}$ union Res$_{B2}$)]
> Otherwise 'Res$_A$ union Res$_B$' is ordinary set union.

3.6.2 Definitions of the result of a satisfied D&Qs formula

(a) A simple QUALIFIER has the empty result.
(b) 'Desc is qual(V,Qual)' has result [Res$_D$ + Res$_Q$], where

> Desc is a DESCRIPTION with result Res$_D$, and
> 'qual(V,Qual)' is a Curried QUALIFIER with result Res$_Q$.

(c) A simple DESCRIPTION (which is just a constant) has the empty result.
(d) 'Det-N-qual(V,Qual)' referring to the group G, has result Res where

> 'qual(V,Qual)' is a Curried QUALIFIER which returns group G' equal to G with the same result, Res.

(e) 'qual(V,Qual)' returning G has result

> $[V \equiv G_1 : \text{Res}_1, V \equiv G_2 : \text{Res}_2, \ldots V \equiv G_n : \text{Res}_n]$ where
> G is the union of $G_1, G_2, \ldots G_n$, and
> the QUALIFIER Qual is satisfied by $V \equiv G_1, X \equiv G_X$ with result Res$_1$
> $V \equiv G_2, X \equiv G_X$ with result Res$_2$
> $\ldots$
> $V \equiv G_n, X \equiv G_X$ with result Res$_n$.

(f) 'Desc$_1$ is funct(V,Desc$_2$)' has result

   [Res$_1$ + [V≡G$_{V1}$: Res$_{21}$, V≡G$_{V2}$: Res$_{22}$, ... V≡G$_{Vn}$: Res$_{2n}$]] where
   the DESCRIPTION Desc$_1$ refers to G with result Res$_1$, and
   G is the union of G$_1$,G$_2$, ...G$_n$ and
   the DESCRIPTION Desc$_2$ is satisfied by

   V≡G$_{V1}$, Y≡G$_Y$ with result Res$_{21}$,
   V≡G$_{V2}$, Y≡G$_Y$ with result Res$_{22}$,
   ...
   V≡G$_{Vn}$, Y≡G$_Y$ with result Res$_{2n}$,

   where each G$_{Vi}$ is equal to G$_i$.

(g) If F$_1$, F$_2$ are both QUALIFIERs or both DESCRIPTIONs, then
   'F$_1$ & F$_2$' has result Res$_1$ union Res$_2$ where Res$_1$ is the result of F$_1$, and
                                                          Res$_2$ is the result of F$_2$.
   'F$_1$ or F$_2$' has result Res where F$_1$ succeeds with result Res, or
                                          F$_2$ succeeds with result Res.

(h) 'not Qual' has the empty result when it succeeds.

3.6.3 Two examples of D&Qs results

Although 'not Qual' has the empty result, a negated query can still yield an answer. Consider, for example the query "Which Berkshire customers do not buy P104's?".

   'what-N-qual(X,customer(name=X,region='berkshire')) is
   qual(Y, not buy(buycust=Y,buyprod='P104')).

The relation 'buy' has only the following relevant tuple,

buy	buycust	buyprod
	'Good Co'	'P104'
	...	...

The relation 'customer' has the same data as in previous examples,

customer	name	region	...
	'Good Co'	'berkshire'	
	'Better Co'	'avon'	
	'Best Co'	'berkshire'	

The result is,

   [[X≡['Best Co'] : [ ]] + Res]

where Res is the result of 'not buy(buycust=Y, buyprod='P104')'.

Although Res is the empty result, [ ], since negated QUALIFIERs always yield the empty result, the whole formula still yields a useful result.

142 SPECIFICATION OF D&Qs [Appendix 2]

One more example is the result of,

'qual(V, any-N-qual(X, true) is qual(Y, customer(name=V, region=Y)))'.

(This Curried QUALIFIER was previously shown to return the set, ['Good Co', 'Better Co', 'Best Co'], in section 2.6 above.) Its result is:

[
    V ≡ ['Better Co'] : [[X ≡ ['avon'] : [ ]] + [Y ≡ ['avon'] : [ ]]],
    V ≡ ['Good Co', 'Best Co'] : [[X ≡ ['berkshire'] : [ ]] + [Y ≡ ['berkshire.] : [ ]]]
].

Appendix 3

A PROLOG program for converting D&Qs to List Commands

1. COMPLEXITY

The program listed here includes all the clauses described in Chapter 4, section 3, although some extra checks have been built in.

This program still cannot deal with the full range of D&Qs because the language is more powerful than these simplified List Commands. For example D&Qs formulae expressing queries with embedded counts ("Who placed two orders in June?") cannot be translated into a single List Command.

(A D&Qs interpreter has been programmed in PROLOG which deals with embedded functions and counts, but there are still D&Qs formulae, such as those involving relations with attributes ranging over ordered lists, which cannot be interpreted. The interpreter suffers from a perennial PROLOG problem of inefficiency, and work is still continuing on the implementation of an efficient D&Qs interpreter in PROLOG).

2. INPUT AND OUTPUT SPECIFICATION

2.1 Specification of D&Qs formula to be input to the converter
(1) Syntax of D&Qs formulae, Appendix 2, section 1 above.
(2) The "Count", as in 'Determiner-Count-qual(V, Qualifier)', is either variable or 1.
(3) No relation is used twice in a formula.

(4) If two DESCRIPTIONs are conjoined ('D1 & D2'), then their references are in the same database domain (see section 2.3 below).
(5) The relations, apart from the built-in relations total, average, etc., have only atom-type attributes.
(6) All variable names are distinct.
(7) The complete query has no free variables.
(8) The results are all within the scope of the database relations ("range quantified"); this ensures that no *variables* occur in the result specification of the List Command.

2.2 Specification of simplified List Commands

List Command	::−	'LIST' Result-Spec 'WHERE' Rule
Result-Spec	::−	Term { ,Result-Spec | nil }
Rule	::−	true | false | Rule & Rule | Rule or Rule | not Rule
Rule	::−	Term Comparison Term
Term	::−	Constant | Relation.Column
Comparison	::−	$>, \geqslant, \leqslant, <, =, \neq$

2.3 Comments

The conjunction of two descriptions is treated disjunctively. Thus "What orders were placed by customers 'C1' and 'C2' ?" has D&Qs interpretation:

> what-N-qual(W1, true) is qual(W2,
> 'C1'&'C2' is qual(X, place(custcode = X, ordercode = W2)))

(where 'place' is the database relation interpreting the verb "to place", which was used in Chapter 4, section 3).

On conversion to a list command this becomes:

> LIST place.custcode, place.ordercode
> WHERE place.custcode='C1' OR place.custcode='C2'

The list command clearly reflects the meaning of the D&Qs formula. It shows how the disjunctive interpretation of 'C1'&'C2' (or in general 'Desc1 & Desc2') works in the conversion of D&Qs to simplified list commands.

3. THE PROLOG PROGRAM

Two of the predicates used in this program are not actually defined. They are 'writeout' and 'error'.

```
?- op(700, xfy, or).
?- op(600, xfy, & ).
?- op(500, xfy, not).
?- op(700, xfy, '.').
```

/* 'not not . . .' undoes all the variable bindings that result from the conversion
/* process. The predicate 'used' is a kind of 'blackboard' for recording which
/* relations have been used in the query. */
convert(DandQs) :− not not conv(DandQs),!,retractall(used(_)).
convert(DandQs):−
       error('Formula could not be converted', DandQs),
       retractall(used(_)).

/* Displays the final list command. */
conv(DandQs) :− convqual(DandQs, Results, Rules),
       write('LIST'),
       writeout(Results),
       write('WHERE'),
       writeout(Rules),nl.

/* Clause as described in Chapter 4, section 3.2.3 except that this version rejects
/* logical combinations of DESCRIPTIONs and adds a final check that the
/* variable is bound. */
convqual (Desc is qual(V, Qual), Results, Rule):−
       not(Desc = (D1 or D2)), not(Desc = (D1 & D2)),!,
       convqual(Qual, Res1, Rule1),
       convdesc(Desc, W, Res2, Rule2),
       substitute(V, W, Rule3),
       union(Res1, Res2, Results),
       conjunct([Rule1, Rule2, Rule3], Rule),
       check(V, Desc is qual(V, Qual)).

convqual (Qual1 & Qual2, Results, Rule) :−
       convqual(Qual1, Res1, Rule1),
       convqual(Qual2, Res2, Rule2),
       union(Res1, Res2, Results),
       conjunct ([Rule1, Rule2], Rule).

/* We could define a predicate 'disjunct', similar to 'conjunct', which would
/* simplify 'Rule or false' to 'Rule'. */

convqual (Qual1 or Qual2, Results, Rule1 or Rule2) :−
       convqual(Qual1, Res1, Rule1),
       convqual(Qual2, Res2, Rule2),
       union(Res1, Res2, Results).

convqual (not Qual1, Results, not Rule) :−
       convqual (Qual1, Results, Rule).

convqual (true, [ ], true) :−!.
convqual (fail, [ ] , false) :−!.

/* Converts simple QUALIFIERs as described in Chapter 4, section 3.2.2 */

convqual (Qual, [ ], Rule) :−
    Qual=. . [Rel|Atts],
    relation (Rel),!, convrel (Rel, Atts, Rule).

/* Converts built-in functions such as 'total', 'average', 'max' and 'min'. */
convqual(Qual, [ ], true) :−
    Qual=. . [Rel | Atts],
    built_in (Rel),!, convfunct (Rel, Atts).

convqual (Qual, _, _) :−
    functor (Qual, Rel, _), Rel\= is, !,
    error('unrecognised relation name', Rel).

check (V,_) :− nonvar (V),!.
check (V, Qualifier) :−
    error ('No constraints on variable', Qualifier).

/* As in Chapter 4, section 3.2.2 */
convrel (Rel, [Att = Rel. Att | Selections], Rule) :−
    !,convrel (Rel, Selections, Rule).

/* An extension to Chapter 4, section 3.2.2 to deal with '>', '<' etc */
convrel(Rel, [Selection | Sel], Rule) :−
    Selection=. . [Comp, Att, Arg],
    Rule1=. . [Comp, Rel.Att, Arg],
    convrel (Rel, Sel, Rule2),
    conjunct ([Rule1,Rule2], Rule).

/* Rejects queries like "What costs more than pencils?". Without this clause this
/* query would yield
/*   "LIST PRODUCT WHERE PRODUCT.UNIT-PRICE >
/*   PRODUCT.UNIT-PRICE AND
/*   PRODUCT.PRODUCTDESC = 'pencils' ".*/
convrel(Rel, [ ],_) :−
    used (Rel),!, error('relation used twice', Rel).

convrel (Rel, [ ], true) :−
    assert (used (Rel)).

convrel(Rel,_,_):− not(retract (used (Rel))).

/* The QUALIFIER 'total(result=X, arguments=Y)' would result in the binding
/* of 'X' to 'total (Y)'. */
convfunct (Funct, [result = X, arguments = Y]) :−
    X=. . [Funct,Y] , !.

/* If 'X' is not itself a variable, the converter gives up. It should only work if 'X'
/* ultimately ends up in the result spec. */
convfunct (Funct,_) :–
	error ('embedded function', Funct).

/* Chapter 4, section 3.2.3 */
convdesc(Const, Const, [ ], true):–
	atomic(Const), !.

/* Already converted. */
convdesc(Rel.Att, Rel.Att, [ ], true):– !.

/* Rejects "Who placed 2 pencils. */
convdesc(Det-N-qual (V, Qual),_,_,_) :–
	nonvar(N), N>1, !,
	error('embedded count', Det-N-qual(V, Qual)).

/* Chapter 4, section 3.2.5 */
convdesc(what-N-qual (V, Qual), W, [V | Results], Rule):–
	convdesc(any-N-qual (V, Qual), W, Results, Rule).

/* Chapter 4, section 3.2.4 */
convdesc (Det-N-qual (V, Qual), V, Results, Rule) :–
	convqual (Qual, Results, Rule).

/* This works because, under the constraints specified in 2.1 above,
/*   '(D1 is funct(V, D2)) is qual(W, Qual)'
/* has the same semantics as
/*   'D1 is qual (V, D2 is qual(W, Qual))'. */
convdesc (D1 is funct(V, D2), W, Results, Rule) :–
	convqual (D1 is qual (V, D2 is qual (W, true)),
		Results,
		Rule).
/* Chapter 4, section 3.2.3 */
substitute(X,X,true):–!.
substitute(X,Y,X=Y).

/* **Messy Bits** */

/* See 2.3, above. */
convqual ((D1 & D2) is qual(V, Qual), Results, Rule) :–
	convqual ((D1 or D2) is qual (V, Qual), Results, Rule).

/* No problem if the conversion of 'Qual' binds 'V'. This clause is just like
/* Chapter 4, section 3.2.3 except that 'substitute' is done within 'convdesc'. */
convqual ((D1 or D2) is qual (V, Qual), Results, Rule) :–

```
        convqual (Qual, Res1, Rule1),
        nonvar (V),
        convdesc (D1 or D2, V, Res2, Rule2),
        union (Res1, Res2, Results),
        conjunct ([Rule1, Rule2], Rule).
```

/* If 'V' is still variable after doing 'convqual', then be careful! */
```
convqual ((D1 or D2) is qual (V, Qual), Results, Rule) :—
        convqual (Qual, Res1, Rule1),
        var (V),
        convdisjunct (D1 or D2, V, Res1, Rule1, Results, Rule).
```

/* See 2.3 above. */
```
convdesc (D1 & D2, W, Results, Rule) :—
        convdesc (D1 or D2, W, Results, Rule).
```

/* Since 'V' is already bound it is not affected by 'substitute', so 'D1' and 'D2' */
/* are dealt with independently. Notice that 'V' is slipped into the result spec.; */
/* thus in 2.3 above, 'place.custcode' gets into the results. */
```
convdesc (D1 or D2, V, Results, (Rule1 or Rule2)) :—
        convdesc (D1, W1, Res1, R1),
        substitute (W1, V, R2),
        conjunct ([R1, R2], Rule1),
        convdesc (D2, W2, Res2, R3),
        substitute (W2, V, R4),
        conjunct ([R3, R4], Rule2),
        union ([V | Res1], Res2, Results).
```

/* 'V1' is variable, and it is assumed that it gets bound by 'convdesc' ('checkdisj' */
/* checks this). Thus every occurrence of 'V1' has to be replaced by 'V2' so that */
/* the DESCRIPTION 'D2' can be converted subsequently. 'V1' is added to the */
/* result spec, 'Res1'. It is likely that 'Res1' and 'Res2' (from the second */
/* conjunct) will have an overlap. Any redundancy should be eliminated by */
/* 'union'. */
```
convdisjunct (D1 or D2, V1, Res1A, R1A, Results, (Rule1 or Rule2)) :— !,
        mk (V1, V2, Res1A, Res2A),
        mk (V1, V2, R1A, R2A),
        convdesc (D1, V1, Res1B, R1B),
        conjunct ([R1A, R1B], Rule1),
        union (Res1A, [V1 | Res1B], Res1),
        checkdisj (V1, D1),
        convdisjunct (D2, V2, Res2A, R2A, Res2, Rule2),
        union (Res1, Res2, Results).
```

/* The last disjunct is converted just as in Chapter 4, section 3.2.3 except that */
/* 'substitute' is done automatically by PROLOG unification. */
```
convdisjunct (Desc, V, Res1, Rule1, Results, Rule) :—
```

```
                    convdesc (Desc, V, Res2, Rule2),
                    conjunct ([Rule1 | Rule2], Rule),
                    union (Res1, Res2, Results),
                    checkdisj (V, Desc).

checkdisj (V1, _ ) :- nonvar (V1), !.
checkdisj (V1, D1) :-
        error ('No constraints on variable in disjunct', D1 is qual (V1, true)).

/* This predicate could be improved (to recognise repeated rules, for example). */
conjunct ([true | Tail], Rule) :-!, conjunct (Tail, Rule).
conjunct ([Rule, true], Rule) :-!.
conjunct ([Rule1, Rule2], Rule1 & Rule2) :-!.
conjunct ([Rule1 | Tail], Rule3) :-!, conjunct (Tail, Rule2),
                                      conjunct ([Rule1, Rule2], Rule3).
conjunct ([ ], true).

/* Union appends two lists dropping duplicated members */
union ([H | T], L1, L2) :- idmemb (H,L1),!,union (T, L1, L2).
union ([H | T], L1, [H | L2]) :-!,union (T,L1, L2).
union ([ ], L, L).

idmemb (H1, [H2 | _ ]) :- H1 = = H2,!.
idmemb (X, [H | Tail]) :- idmemb (X, Tail).

/* Finally two nasty little predicates that unpick PROLOG structures, replace
/* 'V1' with 'V2' wherever it occurs, and put them together again. */

mk (V1, V2, W1, V2)    :- V1 = = W1, !.
mk (V1, V2, X, X)      :- (atomic (X); var (X)), !.
mk (V1, V2, W1, W2)    :- W1 = .. [H | T1], m1 (V1, V2, T1, T2),
                          W2 = .. [H | T2].

m1 (V1, V2, [H1 | T1], [H2 | T2]) :- !,mk (V1, V2, H1, H2), ml (V1, V2, T1, T2).
ml (_,_, [ ], [ ]).
```

Appendix 4

The election and COPSE databases

1. THE QPROC ELECTION DATABASE

1.1 Domains

Built-in Domains:
  date
  location
  measure
  person
  thing

Entity Domains:
  constituency
  election
  marginality
  (person)

Other Domains:
  area
  party
  title
  vote
  year

1.2 Domain hierarchy

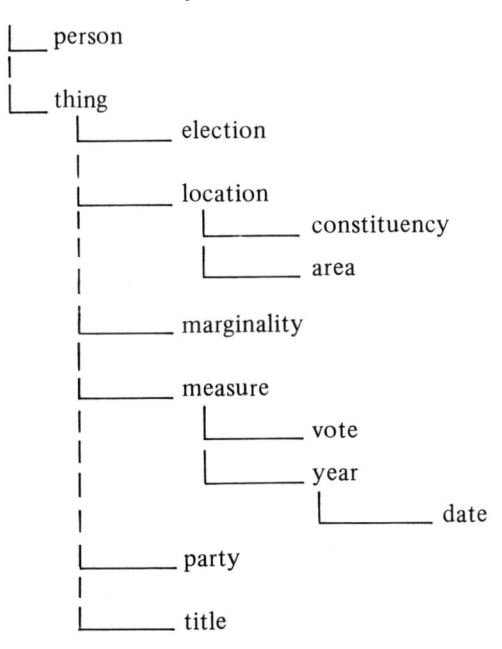

```
|__ person
|
|__ thing
        |_____ election
        |
        |_____ location
        |         |_____ constituency
        |         |
        |         |_____ area
        |
        |_____ marginality
        |
        |_____ measure
        |         |_____ vote
        |         |
        |         |_____ year
        |                 |_____ date
        |
        |_____ party
        |
        |_____ title
```

1.3 Relations

Relation:	Attribute:	Domain:
person	id	person
person	age	year
person	title	title
constituency	id	constituency
constituency	area	area
constituency	marginality	marginality
constituency	member	person
election	id	election
election	constituency	constituency
election	date	date
marginality	id	marginality
marginality	party	party
candidate	candidate	person
candidate	election	election
candidate	vote	vote
candidate	party	party

1.4 Entities
There are four entities

Relation Name:	Identifying Attribute:	Domain:
person	id	person
election	id	election
constituency	id	constituency
marginality	id	marginality

1.5 Verbs

Derived Relation:	Derived From:
contest	candidate election
win	candidate election
lose	candidate election constituency

2. THE COPSE (CUSTOMERS, ORDERS, PRODUCTS AND STOCK ENQUIRIES) DATABASE
2.1 Domains

Built-in Domains:
   date
   location
   measure
   person
   thing

Entity Domains:
   customer
   product
   order
   salesman
   stock

Other Domains:

name	description
address1	money
address2	postcode
bin	region
quantity	warehouse
county	

2.2 Domain hierarchy

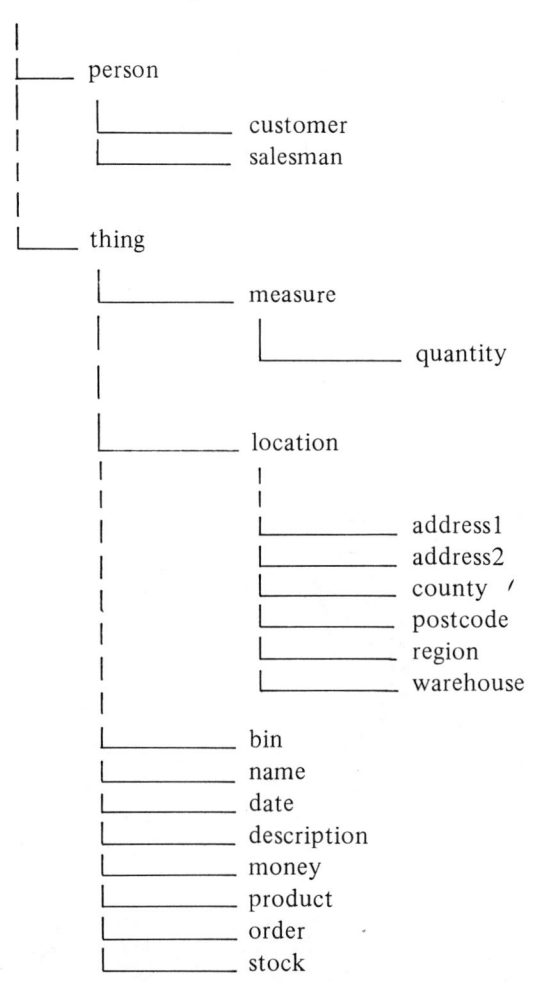

```
|
|____ person
|       |
|       |_____ customer
|       |_____ salesman
|
|____ thing
        |
        |_____ measure
        |           |
        |           |_____ quantity
        |
        |_____ location
        |           |
        |           |_____ address1
        |           |_____ address2
        |           |_____ county
        |           |_____ postcode
        |           |_____ region
        |           |_____ warehouse
        |
        |_____ bin
        |_____ name
        |_____ date
        |_____ description
        |_____ money
        |_____ product
        |_____ order
        |_____ stock
```

2.3 Relations

Relation:	Attribute:	Domain:
customer	id	customer
	custname	name
	address1	address1
	address2	address2
	county	county
	postcode	postcode
	creditlimit	money
	balance	money
	smannumber	salesman

Relation:	Attribute:	Domain:
product	id	product
	productdesc	description
	unitprice	money
	unitofissue	quantity
order	id	order
	orderdate	date
	customer	customer
orderline	productorder	product
	order	order
	quantity	quantity
salesman	id	salesman
	name	name
	region	region
stock	id	stock
	productstock	product
	stockwhse	warehouse
	binid	bin
	qtyonhand	quantity
	reorderlevel	quantity
	reorderqty	quantity

2.4 Entities

Relation name:	Identifying Attribute:	Domain:
customer	id	customer
order	id	order
product	id	product
salesman	id	salesman
stock	id	stock

2.5 Verbs

Derived relation:	Derived from:
cost	product
contain	orderline
hold	stock
place	order
serve	customer
buy	customer
	order
	orderline
	salesman

Derived relation:	Derived from:
order2	orderline order customer
take	order customer
worth1	stock product
worth2	orderline product

Appendix 5

Introduction to PROLOG

1. OVERVIEW

PROLOG is an interactive programming language based on logic. An excellent introduction to the language is in [30].

The user runs a program by entering a 'goal' (which is a logical formula) and the system executes the program by searching for a proof of the formula.

At any time the PROLOG system has a database of 'clauses' (which are logical theorems) from which to prove goals entered by the user.
For example, with the clauses:

        office_equipment(desk).
        office_equipment(X) :— stationery(X).
        stationery(pen).

the PROLOG system can prove the goals

        ?- office_equipment(desk).
        ?- office_equipment(pen).

2. SYNTAX

The clauses are either 'facts', like

    office_equipment(desk).
    stationery(pen).

or 'rules', like

    office_equipment(X) :— stationery(X).

[Appendix 5] INTRODUCTION TO PROLOG 157

More complicated clauses are possible such as:

part_of(car, engine)

This is another fact. It has a 'predicate', "part-of", and two arguments, "car" and "engine".

component(X,Y) :− part(X), part(Y), part_of(X,Y).

This is another rule. It has a 'head', "component(X,Y)" and a 'body'. The body consists of three 'goals', part(X), part(Y), part_of(X,Y).

component(X,Y) :− part_of(X,Z), component(Z,Y)

There is a rule whose body contains a goal "component(Z,Y)" which matches its head, "component(X,Y)". Such recursive rules can lead to non-terminating proofs.

A 'fact', a 'head' and a 'goal' all have the same structure. They are PROLOG 'terms'. This enables PROLOG clauses to be used also as data. Thus a PROLOG 'term' may be called as a 'goal', asserted as a 'clause' or used as a component of another term.

A PROLOG term is a

Constant
Variable
or Structure

A constant may be an integer or an atom. Atoms may begin with a lowercase letter, e.g.

fred
old_age,

or else they may consist entirely of symbols, e.g.

:−
+

or finally they may have any characters enclosed in single quotes, e.g.

'2'
'This Appendix'

A variable begins with a capital letter (or an underline),

Fred
_fred

The anonymous variable

_

is used when an identifying name is not required (i.e. the variable is only mentioned once).

A structure is written in PROLOG by specifying its 'functor' (which is an atom) and its 'components' (which are terms). The components are enclosed in round brackets and separated by commas:

>part_of(X,engine)
>manager(employee('Smith'),employee('Jones'),project('London', proj01)).

PROLOG clauses can be read 'declaratively' — like a logical assertion — or 'procedurally'.

>A :— B, C, D.

is expressed declaratively as

>"A is true if B, C and D are true",

and is expressed procedurally as

"To satisfy goal A, satisfy goal B, then goal C, then goal D".

To read PROLOG clauses it is important to understand about 'operators'. An operator is simply a functor that is allowed to appear between its components. Thus if "part_of" is an operator it can be written *either* as

>part_of(X,Y)

or as

>X part_of Y

Any functor can be declared as an operator by calling the goal (e.g.):

>?- op(800,xfy,part_of).

/* This is a comment:
/* Defines "part_of" as an infix operator with precedence 800. */

PROLOG includes some built-in clauses. For example, ";" is defined by an infix operator meaning "or". "true" is defined as a logical theorem. Thus the following clauses are built-in:

>?- op(1100, xfy,';').
>(A ; B) :— A.
>(A ; B) :— B.
>true.

In fact ':—' is just another operator, and a rule

>A :— Body

can equally be written ':—' (A,Body).

One final syntactic structure is used for lists.

[ ] is an atom representing the empty list. As in LISP, lists can be constructed by the 'dot' operator:

    first.(second.(third.(fourth.[ ])))

However, this can also be expressed in PROLOG using square brackets.

    [first, second, third, fourth]

A vertical bar can be used to mark the tail of the list, e.g.

    [first, second | Tail]

("Tail" is a variable ranging over lists), or

    [first, second | [third, fourth]]

3. PROCEDURAL SEMANTICS

A typical predicate dealing with lists is 'append', which appends two lists to yield an appended list.

    append([H|X], Y, [H|Z]) :– append (X,Y,Z).
    append([ ], Y, Y).

This states that a list with head "H" and tail "Z" results from appending a list "Y" to a list with head "H" and tail "X", if "Z" results from appending "Y" to "X". Moreover, the result of appending a list "Y" to the empty list is "Y" itself.

If the user enters the goal:

    ?- append([a, b], [c,d], List).

the interpreter matches it against the head of the first clause *instantiating* the variables H, X and Y to 'a', [b] and [c,d] respectively.

The partially instantiated list [a|Z] is substituted into "List", so that when Z is finally instantiated, List will become instantiated too.

It then attempts to prove the goal

    ?- append ([b], [c,d], Z)

This also matches the first clause, but the variables are local to the clause instance so that a new H, X, Y and Z (we shall call them H2, X2, Y2 and Z2) are created and we can rewrite the clauses for 'append' as:

    append([H2|X2], Y2, [H2|Z2]) :–
        append(X2, Y2, Z2).
    append([ ], Y2, Y2).

    H2 is instantiated to b
    X2 is instantiated to [ ] (because [b]=[b|[ ]])
    Y2 is instantiated to [c,d]

and finally, Z is 'unified' with the partially instantiated list [b|Z2].

The interpreter then goes on to try the goal

?- append ([ ], [c,d], Z2)

which does not match the first clause but only the second. Its effect is to instantiate Z2 to the list [c,d]. Thus

Z becomes [b,c,d] and
List becomes [a,b,c,d].

This completes the successful execution of the goal

?-append ([a,b], [c,d], List).

Notice that a PROLOG goal is like a procedure where each parameter can be used for input or output. Thus the goal

?- append(X, Y, [a,b,c,d]).

also succeeds instantiating X to [a,b,c,d] and Y to [ ].

However, the PROLOG interpreter also has the facility to change its mind if a proof does not work first time. This facility can be exampled by following a proof of

?- append(List, [a], [a]).

Again this matches the first clause for 'append' unifying 'List' with [H|X], instantiating Y to [a], H to a and Z to [ ]. (Thus List becomes [a|X]).

The interpreter then tries the goal

?- append(X, [a], [ ]).

This does not match the first goal (because the empty list cannot match [H|Z]), nor the second because if Y is instantiated to [a], it cannot also instantiate to [ ].

The PROLOG interpreter therefore 'backtracks', undoes the substitutions and looks for an alternative to the previous match.

Instead of matching

append(List, [a], [a])

with the head of the first clause, it matches it with the second clause. This instantiates List to [ ] and the goal succeeds at once.

All this power in the interpreter can lead to problems. An example is the goal

?- append(X, [ ], Z).

Ideally, this would simply result in the substitution of X for Z. In practice, however, it causes a loop because, after matching the goal with the head of the first clause for append, the interpreter will then attempt to prove the goal.

?- append(X2, [ ], Z2)

which is the same as the initial goal.

Here is an informal definition of PROLOG's procedural semantics (from Warren and Pereira [50]):

To *execute* a goal, the system searches [the PROLOG 'database'] for the first clause whose head *matches* or *unifies* with the goal. The *unification* process finds the most general common instance of the two terms, which is unique if it exists. If a match is found, the matching clause instance is then *activated* by executing in turn, from left to right, each of the goals (if any) in its body. If at any time the system fails to find a match for a goal, it *backtracks,* i.e. it rejects the most recently activated clause, undoing any substitutions made by the match with the head of the clause. Next it reconsiders the original goal which activated the rejected clause, and tries to find a subsequent clause which also matches the goal.

4. BUILT-IN PREDICATES

To understand the PROLOG programs in this book, it is necessary to know the semantics of some of PROLOG's built-in predicates.

When such a predicate is called as a goal, instead of attempting a proof, the interpreter enters a subroutine. The relevant predicates are

write	nonvar
assert	var
retract	atomic
retractall	==
op	!
call	not
=..	true
functor	fail

write(X)	writes X to the output and succeeds.
assert(X)	takes a term X, asserts it as a clause in the PROLOG database, and succeeds.
retract(X)	removes X from the database and succeeds. If there is no matching clause it fails.
retractall(X)	retracts all facts and rules whose head matches X. It succeeds if there are none.
op(Prec, xfy, Op)	defines an infix operator, Op, with precedence Prec.
call(X)	calls the term, X, as a goal and succeeds if X does.
X=..[F|Args]	takes a structure 'X' and unpicks it into a list containing its functor, F, and its components, e.g.

part(car,engine)=..[part,car,engine]

Alternatively, it takes a list and creates a structure.

functor(X, Functor, No)	takes a structure X and extracts it functor "Functor" and its number of components "No". Alternatively, given Functor and No it creates X.
var(X)	succeeds if X is a variable. Otherwise it fails.
nonvar(X)	succeeds if an only if var(X) fails.
atomic(X)	succeeds if X is a constant, otherwise it fails.
X==Y	succeeds if X and Y are identical. If X and Y are unifiable, but distinct, it still fails.
!	This is PROLOG's most controversial feature. It is a directive to the interpreter to remove all alternative choices since the parent goal. A typical example is the placing of a cut after the terminating clause for append:

?- append([ ], Y, Y) :−!.
?- append([H|X], Y, [H|Z]) :− append(X,Y,Z).

This prevents the interpreter looping on

?- append([a|T], [ ], Z), Z = [b].

for example, but causes

?- append(X, Y, Z), X = [a].

to fail, thus destroying **PROLOG**'s declarative semantics.

not — the semantics of 'not' is linked with '!', its semantics being equivalent to:

not(X) :− call(X), !, fail.
not(X).

not(not(X)) succeeds if X does, but without performing any substitutions.

true	succeeds always.
fail	fails.

References

[1] Abrial, J. R. *Data Semantics,* Proc. IFIP TC-2 Working Conf. on Database Management Systems, April 1974. Ed. Klimbie, J. W. and Koffeman, K. L., North-Holland.

[2] Berry-Rogghe, G. L., Kolvenback, M., and Lutre, H. D., 'Interacting with PLIDIS a deductive question answering system for German', pp. 138–216 in *Natural Language Question Answering Systems,* ed. L. Bolc, Carl Hanser Verlag, 1980.

[3] Bruce, B. 'Case systems for natural language', *Artificial Intelligence,* **6**, 4, Winter 1975, 327–360.

[4] Chomsky, N. *Aspects of the Theory of Syntax,* MIT Press, 1965.

[5] Codd, E. F. 'Seven steps to rendezvous with the casual user', Proc. IFIP TC-2 Working Conf. on Database Management Systems, April 1974. Ed. Klimbie, J. W. and Koffeman, K. L., North-Holland.

[6] Colmerauer, A. 'An interesting natural language subset', Groupe d'Intelligence Artificielle, Univ. of Marseille, Luminy, Marseille, Oct. 1977.

[7] Cuff, R. N. 'Database query systems for the casual user', IBM Research Laboratory, Hursley, Winchester, Hants, 1979.

[8] Artificial Intelligence Corp. *INTELLECT Query System User's Guide,* 500 Fifth Ave, Waltham, Mass. 02254, 1980.

[9] Dahl, V. Ph.D.Thesis, Univ. of Marseille, Luminy, Marseille, 1977.

[10] Dahl, V. 'Logical design of deductive natural language consultable databases', Proc. 5th Conference on Very Large Databases, Rio de Janeiro, 1979.

[11] Fillmore, C. J. 'The case for case', pp. 1–90 in *Universals in Linguistic Theory,* ed. Bach and Harms, Holt, Rinehart and Winston, New York, 1968.

[12] Finin, T., Goodman, G. and Tennant, H. 'JETS: Achieving completeness through coverage and closure', Working Paper 19, Advanced Automation Group, Coordinated Science Lab., Univ. of Illinois, Urbana, Ill., 1979.
[13] Finin, T. W. 'The semantic interpretation of nominal compounds', Proc. Int. Joint Conf. on Artificial Intelligence, Aug. 1979.
[14] Gallaire, H. and Minker, J. *Logic and Databases,* Plenum Press, 1978.
[15] Ginsparg, J. M. 'A robust portable natural language database interface', Proc. Conf. on Applied Nat. Lang. Proc., Santa Monica, 1–3 Feb. 1983.
[16] Goodman, B. A. 'A model for a natural language database system', Report R-798, Univ. of Illinois, Urbana, Ill., Oct. 1977.
[17] Grice, H. P. 'Logic and conversation', pp. 41–58 in *Syntax and Semantics* Vol. 3, ed. Cole, P. and Morgan, J. L., Academic Press, 1975.
[18] Grosz, B. J. 'The representation and use of focus in a system for understanding dialogues', Proc. 5th Int. Joint Conf. on Artificial Intelligence, 1977, pp. 67–76.
[19] Grosz, B. J. 'TEAM: A transportable natural language interface system', Proc. Conf. on Applied Nat. Lang. Proc., Santa Monica, 1–3 Feb. 1983.
[20] Hadden, G. D. 'NETEDI: An augmented transition network editor', Report T-49, Univ. of Illinois, Urbana, Ill., July 1977.
[21] Harris, L. R., 'The ROBOT system: Natural language processing applied to database query', TR78-1, Maths. Dept., Dartmouth College, Hanover, New Hampshire, Oct. 1978.
[22] Hendrix, G. G., Sacerdoti, E. D., Sagalowicz, D., and Slocum, J. 'Developing a natural language interface to complex data', *ACM TODS,* **3**, 2, June 1978, 105–147.
[23] Hirst, G. 'Anaphora in natural language understanding: A survey', *Lecture Notes In Computer Science,* 119, Springer Verlag, 1981.
[24] 'Using Querymaster (200 level)', ICL Technical Publication, 1983.
[25] Kaplan, S. J. 'Special section – Natural language', *ACM SIGART Newsletter,* Jan. 1982, pp. 27–109.
[26] Kelly, M. J. and Chapanis, A. 'Limited vocabulary natural language dialogue', *Int. Journal Man–Machine Studies,* **9**, 1977, 479–501.
[27] King, M. 'Mutatis Mutandis I', Working Paper No. 30, Institute for Semantic and Cognitive Studies, Univ. of Geneva, 1976.
[28] King, M., Dell'Orco, P., and Spadavecchia, V. N. 'Catering for the experienced and the naive user', Proc. Workshop on Natural Language for Interaction with Databases, International Institute for Applied Systems Analysis, 1977.
[29] McCord, M. C. 'Using slots and modifiers in logic grammars for natural language', *Artificial Intelligence,* **18**, 3, May 1982.
[30] Mellish, C. S. and Clocksin, W. F. *Programming in PROLOG,* Springer Verlag, 1981.
[31] Moore, R. C. 'Problems in logical form', 19th Annual Meeting of the ACL, Stanford, June–July 1981.

REFERENCES

[32] Mylopoulos, J. and Wong, H. K. T. 'Some features of the TAXIS data model', Proc. Conf. on Very Large Databases, 1980, pp. 399–410.

[33] Parisi, D. and Antinucci, F. *Essentials of Grammar,* translated by Bates, E., Academic Press, 1976.

[34] Pereira, F. C. N. 'Extraposition grammars', Logic Programming Workshop, Debrecen, Hungary, July 1980, Proceedings ed. Tarnlund, S.-A., pp. 231–242.

[35] Perrault, C. R., Allen, J. F., and Cohen, P. R. 'Speech acts as a basis for understanding dialogue coherence', Theoretical Issues in Natural Language Processing, July 1978, Proceedings ed. Waltz, D. L., pp. 125–132.

[36] Petrick, J. R., 'Theoretical/technical issues in natural language access to databases' Proc. 20th Annual Meeting of ACL, Toronto, June 1982.

[37] Quine, W. V. 'The vagaries of definition', in *Ways of Paradox,* Harvard Univ. Press, 1966.

[38] Sabatier, P. Ph.D. Thesis, Univ. of Marseille, Luminy, Marseille, 1980.

[39] Schank, R. C. (ed.) *Conceptual Information Processing,* North-Holland, 1975.

[40] Shieber, S. M. and Ronsenshein, S. J. 'Translating English into logical form', Proc. 20th Annual Meeting of the ACL, Toronto, June 1982.

[41] Sidner, C. L. 'The use of focus as a tool for disambiguation of definite noun phrases', Theoretical Issues in Natural Language Processing, July 1978, Proceedings ed. Waltz, D. L., pp. 86–95.

[42] Siklóssy, L. 'Impertinent question-answering systems: Justification and Theory', Proc. ACM Annual Conf., Washington DC, Dec. 1978, pp. 39–44.

[43] Sparck Jones, K. and Boguraev, B. 'How to drive a database front end using general semantic information', Proc. Conf. on Applied Nat. Lang. Proc., Santa Monica, 1–3 Feb. 1983.

[44] Templeton, M. and Burger, J. 'Problems in natural language interface to DBMS with examples from EUFID', Proc. Conf. on Applied Nat. Lang. Proc., Santa Monica, 1–3 Feb. 1983.

[45] Tennant, H. 'Experience with the evaluation of natural language question answerers', Advanced Automation Group, Coordinated Science Lab., Univ. of Illinois, Urbana, Ill., 1979.

[46] Thompson, F. B. and Thompson, B. H. 'Rapidly extensible natural language', Proc. ACM Annual Conf. Washington DC, 1978, pp. 178–182.

[47] Thompson, F. B. and Thompson, B. H. 'Shifting to a higher gear in a natural language system', AFIPS NCC Conference Proceedings, 1981, pp. 657–662.

[48] Thompson, F. B. and Thompson, B. H. 'Introducing ASK, a simple knowledgeable system', Proc. Conf. on Applied Nat. Lang. Proc., Santa Monica, 1–3 Feb. 1983.

[49] Waltz, D. L., Finin, T., Green, F., Conrad, F., Goodman, B. and Hadden, G. 'The PLANES system: Natural language access to a large database', Report T-34, Univ. of Illinois, Urbana, Ill., Nov. 1976.

[50] Warren, D. H. D. and Pereira, F. C. N. 'Definite clause grammars for language analysis − A survey of the formalism and a comparison with augmented transition networks', *Artificial Intelligence,* **13**, 3, May 1980.

[51] Webber, B. L. and Reiter, R. 'Anaphora and logical form: On formal meaning representations for English', Proc. 5th Int. Joint Conf. on Artificial Intelligence, MIT, 1977, pp. 121−131.

[52] Wilks, Y. 'An intelligent analyser and understander of English', *Comm. ACM,* **18**, 1975, 264−274.

[53] Wilks, Y. 'A preferential pattern-seeking semantics for natural language inference', *Artificial Intelligence,* **6**, 1, Spring 1975, 53−74.

[54] Wilks, Y. 'Natural language understanding systems within the AI paradigm − A survey and some comparisons', Stanford A.I. Lab., Memo 237, Stanford Univ., Stanford, California, 1975.

[55] Wilks, Y. and Charniak, E. 'Computational semantics', in *Fundamental Studies in Computer Science,* Vol. 4, North-Holland, 1976.

[56] Winograd, T. *Understanding Natural Language,* Academic Press, New York, 1972.

[57] Winograd, T. *Language as a Cognitive Process,* Vol. 1, *Syntax,* Appendix B, Addison-Wesley, 1983.

[58] Woods, W. A. 'Transition network grammars for natural language analysis', *Comm. ACM,* **13**, Oct. 1970, 591−606.

[59] Woods, W. A. 'Semantics and quantification in natural language question answering', pp. 1−87 in *Advances in Computers,* Vol. 17, Academic Press, New York, 1978.

[60] Zadeh, L. A. 'PRUF − A meaning representation language for natural languages', *Int. Journal of Man−Machine Studies,* **10**, 1978, 395−460.

[61] Zloof, M. M. 'Query by example: A database language', *IBM Systems Journal,* No. 4, 1977, 324−343.

Index

Page numbers in italic indicate that the entry appears in a heading on that page.

active, *see* passive and active
adjective, 43, 83, 99, 129
adverb, 83
adverbial clauses, 43
adviser, 12
algebra, *see* relational algebra
ambiguity, 20, 45, *50*
anaphora 33, 34, 38
    identity of reference (IRA), identity of sense (ISA), 36, 37, 42
antonymy, 31
applicability, *see* restrictions
application independence, *see* portability
arguments, PROLOG, 157
article, 83, 98
ASK, 38, 39
association, 61, 135
atom, *66*, 135
attribute, 31, *61*, 123
augmented transition network (ATN), *see* transition network
augmentation, 21, 116, 117

backtracking, 22, 160
bag, *66*, 136
Bari, 27, 44
benefactive case, 86
body, PROLOG, 157
BROWSER, 47
builder, natural language interface, 16
built-in vocabulary, *see* vocabulary, basic

calculus, *see* relational calculus
case, grammatical, 87, *90*
case analysis, 29, 52
classifier, 43, 83, 99
clause, *84*, 93
clause, PROLOG, 156
COBOL, 49
CODASYL, 17, 39, 123
communication, verbal and teletype, 110
comparison operators, 61, 134
complements, 83
completeness, 13, 47
component, PROLOG, 158
componential analysis, 91, 112, 113
concepts, underlying, *see* componential analysis
conceptual dependency, 27, 44
conjunctions, 93, 137, 139
content words, 21, 30, 109
context, *33*, 109
continuation, 114
'conv', 81
converting D&Qs, *71*
COPSE database, *152*
core dictionary, *see* dictionary core
core qualifier, *see* qualifier core
count 83, 98
coverage, 28
Currying, *59*

data model, *see* modelling, data

168 INDEX

database management system (DBMS) 43, 122, 123
D&Qs, *53, 56, 133*
declarative, *40*
declarative sentence, 83
deep structure, *51*
definition, *28*
degree-of-strictness, grammar, 109
derived relations, *see* relations, base and derived
DESCRIPTION, *53, 58,* 63, 66, 98, 133
Description, *53, 58,* 63, 66, 98, 133
  definite, 70, 71
determiner, *see also* article, 118, 131
  formal, 53, *69,* 134
dialogue, 48, 127
dictionary
  data, 15, 62, *113,* 128, 131
  English, *29*
  core, *see also* vocabulary, basic, 27, 128
direct object case, 86
domain, 39, 85, 107
  built-in, 95
domain hierarchy, 31, *95*

election database, *150*
ellipsis, *33,* 109
entity, 18, 39, *94,* 123
entity relation, 94
EUFID, 38, 43
European Economic Community, 11
events, 37, 92, 111, 125
expert systems, 12

fact, PROLOG, 156
fall back, mode of parsing, 109
field, 31
fifth generation project, 62
formal query language, 15, *40,*
focus, 129
frames, 38
France, 621
free variable, 135
front end, 12, 121ff.
functor, PROLOG, 158
function, *see* mathematical function
function words, 21, 29, 109
functions, natural language, *63, 103,* 137

generation, natural language, 12, 126
German, 121
Goal, PROLOG, 156
graphics, 126
grammar compiler, *see* parser, PROLOG
grammar rule, PROLOG, 84
'group', 68
  equality and union, 68

habitability, *14*
head, PROLOG, 157
head noun, 43, 83, 98
Hungary, 62
hyponymy, 31, 95

'id', 67, 106, 107
identifying attribute, 94, 95
idiom, 114
imperative, 83
incompatability, 31
incremental, 14
inflexion, 114
informational, *see* restrictions
instantiation, 42, 159
'instrument' case, 87
INTELLECT, *26,* 30, 32, 43, 111, 121, 126
intelligence, 22, 43, 47
intelligent terminal, 126
interrogative, 83

Japan, 62, 121
Jets, 47
joins, 123
  implicit, 94, 95, 123

keyword, 124
knowledge engineer, 112
KRL, 39

LADDER, 22, 43
lambda abstraction, *see* Currying
left recursion, 117
LIFER, *21,* 30, 32, 35
list,
  D&Qs, *66,* 136
  PROLOG, 159
list command, *see* RDBMS, 'list commands'
looping, 160
LUNAR, 33, 34, 38, 39

matching, domains, 95, 102
mathematical function, 55
menu system, 126
meta data and 'metaquestions', 46, 109, *124*
microcomputer, 127
modelling, data, 17, 31, *38,* 56, *94*
MRL, *41*

names, initials, first names and surnames, 110, 111
negation, 140
NETEDI, *28*
networking, *126*
normal form, 96
noun, 83
  proper, 84, 97
  modifier, 98, 99, 103, 130

noun phrase, 83, *97*
    simple, *97*
    compound, 83, *97*
    definite, 33, *35*, 125, 131
null case, 89

objective case, 52
object, data, 39
object, direct and indirect, 43
    see also direct object case
operator, PROLOG, 65, 134, 158

packages, software, 12, 126
paraphrase, *28*, 125
parse tree, 51
parser, *21*
    PROLOG, 116, 128
passive and active, 83, 85
pattern, 18
PLANES, *22*, 28, 32, 34, 38, 43
PLANNER, 37, *40*
PLIDIS, 53, 121
possessive, 83
postmodifier, *101, 103*, 105
postqualifier, *101, 105*
portability, 16, 112, 116
pragmatics, *44, 51*
'predicate', 56
    PROLOG, 157
    built-in, *161*
predicate calculus, 42, 56, 125
predication, 92, 111, 112
preference semantics, 27, 38, 44, 45
preposition, 129
prepositional phrase, 83, 99
preset values, 33, 36
presupposition failure, 54, 70, 71, 125
probable and possible events, 112
procedural, 40, *159*
production, 21, 116
pro-adjectives, pro-acts and pro-verbs, 37
PROLOG, *62*, 118ff, *156*
PROLOG database, 49, 62, 108, 128
PROLOG, Unix, 108
pronouns, 36ff., 61, 121
property, 18
PRUF, 32

QPROC, *48, 108*, 128ff.
QUALIFIER, *53*, 66, 133
    compound, *139*
    Curried, 60, 66, *136*
    simple, 61, *135*
qualifier, core, 100, 101, 104, 119
qualification, attributive and restrictive, 101, 103
qualifying phrases, 20, 26
quantification, 34, 41

quantifier hierarchy, *see also* scope, quantifier, 54, 55
query by example, 12
query language, *see* formal query language
QUERYMASTER, 66

RDBMS 'list commands', *71*
'recipient' case, 88
record, 31, 39
recursion, *see also* Left recursion, 157
reference of a DESCRIPTION, *136*
reference
    anaphoric, *see* anaphora
    evaluation, 55
    pronominal, 33, *36*
    relations, 36
REL, *26, 28,* 43
relations, 31, *61,* 88
    base and derived, *96*
    binary, 26, 127
relational data model, 31, 38, 39, 61, 94, 123
relational algebra and calculus, 40, 94
relationships, 123
relative clause, 43, 83, 98, 103, 105, 130
restrictions, structural, informational, applicability, 17, *18, 19,* 26, 38, 43, 83
result specification, 'list command', 72ff.
results, D&Qs, *71, 140*
'retrieve', 63
ROBOT, 26
rule, 'list command', 72ff.
rule, PROLOG, 156
runtime components of QPROC, *115*

satisfaction, 61, *68, 135, 136*
scope
    quantifier, 51ff.
    variable, 59, 64
segment, 31
selection, 61, 135
semantic category, 97, 98, 101, 104, 107
semantic grammar, *26*
semantic nets, 38
semantic primitives, *see* componential analysis
semantics, *31, 82,*
set, D&Qs, 67, 135
set, CODASYL, 31
shorthand, 27
SHRDLU, 34ff., 40, 124
speech acts, 16, 46
spelling correction, *32*
spoken language, 12, 126
structural, *see* restrictions
sub-entity, 40
subsets, natural language, 11, 15
substitute, *33*
synonym, 31, 113, 114, 122, 124, 125

syntax
    D&Qs, *64*, 133
    formalism, 65, 133, *134*

term, predicate calculus, 56, 58
term, PROLOG, 157
Terse queries, 109
Text, 12, 17
'total' 67
TQA, 38
trace, grammatical, 105
trace, PROLOG, 75ff.,
transition network, 22ff.
transition tree, 22
translation, language, 11
tuple, 61, 100

unification, 159ff.

unix, 108
update, database, *125*
unrecognised words, 132

values, data, 39, 113
verb, 27, 29, 43, 84
    main, 83
    modifiers, 83, *84*, *91*, 93, 129
    'to be', *106*, 129
    vocabulary entry, 88ff.
vertical systems, *124*
vocabulary
    basic, 110, 113
    full, 113, *114*
    limited, 110

who, where, when, etc., 44, 95